de la warr pavilion

**de la warr
pavilion**

de la warr pavilion

the modernist masterpiece

alastair fairley
foreword by richard rogers

MERRELL
LONDON · NEW YORK

First published 2006 by
Merrell Publishers Limited

Head office
81 Southwark Street
London SE1 0HX

New York office
49 West 24th Street, 8th Floor
New York, NY 10010

merrellpublishers.com

in association with

De La Warr Pavilion
Marina
Bexhill on Sea
East Sussex TN40 1DP

dlwp.com

Publisher:
Hugh Merrell

Editorial Director:
Julian Honer

US Director:
Joan Brookbank

Sales and Marketing Manager:
Kim Cope

Sales and Marketing Executive:
Sarah Unitt

US Sales and Marketing Assistant:
Elizabeth Choi

Managing Editor:
Anthea Snow

Project Editors:
Claire Chandler
Rosanna Fairhead

Editor:
Helen Miles

Art Director:
Nicola Bailey

Designer:
Paul Shinn

Production Manager:
Michelle Draycott

Production Controller:
Sadie Butler

British Library Cataloguing-in-
Publication Data:
Fairley, Alastair
De La Warr Pavilion:
the Modernist masterpiece
1. De La Warr Pavilion
(Bexhill, Sussex, England) – History
2. Multipurpose buildings – England –
Bexhill
I. Title
725.8'042'094225

ISBN 1 85894 283 7 (hardback)
ISBN 1 85894 284 5 (paperback)

Project managed for the De La Warr
Pavilion by Celia Davies, Head of
Exhibitions

Designed by John and Orna Designs

Picture research by Sophia Gibb

Copy-edited by Mary Scott

Proof-read by Sarah Yates

Indexed by Christine Shuttleworth

Printed and bound in China

Jacket/cover: South exterior of the De La
Warr Pavilion, photographed in 2006
by Bridget Smith.

The image on pp. 8–9 shows the south
exterior of the De La Warr Pavilion,
photographed in 2005 by Bridget Smith.

The grid used in the background of this
book reflects the scale and proportion
of the De La Warr Pavilion's exterior, and
the curved lines reflect the design of the
interior. The layout aims to convey
the horizontal feel of the building and
its relationship with the landscape.

contents

foreword

The De La Warr Pavilion, standing proud on the coastline of East Sussex, is one of the great Modernist buildings of the twentieth century. It has had, and continues to have, a profound architectural as well as spiritual impact on architects of my generation and on others who will continue the Modernist traditions into the future. As a building it proved to be both a model of collaboration for its architects, Erich Mendelsohn and Serge Chermayeff, and an enigmatic symbol of a European movement that went on to influence the work and teaching of others worldwide.

This book clearly demonstrates the status of the De La Warr Pavilion architecturally; moreover, it amplifies the building's importance and meaning to those who have enjoyed, and those who continue to enjoy, its social and cultural significance. While its history to date has been chequered, with various changes to and demands made on the building over the years and, of course, the pressures that nature and geography have put on it, the pavilion remains a building for the people. The vision and determination of the 9th Earl De La Warr to commission such a building in 1933 still stand today as an exemplar for us to respect and follow.

It is fitting that the history of the pavilion has been articulated in this way, telling the story of the lives of those people who were important to its creation, as well as those who have experienced being there and taking part in its journey.

I wholeheartedly applaud those who have now created the next chapter in the pavilion's history, and who, importantly, have stood fast in bringing its original vision and spirit into the twenty-first century for all to enjoy.

Richard Rogers

director's preface

This book is symbolic of a significant new era for the De La Warr Pavilion. It not only represents the rich history upon which this new era is founded but also reflects the aspirations and sheer determination of a large number of people, each of whom I must wholeheartedly thank.

My gratitude first and foremost goes to the many people who, over many years, campaigned to win national recognition for the pavilion as a Modernist icon and to begin the long process of its repair and redevelopment. In particular, I must thank Jan Wicks, Jill Theis, Peter Evenden, Margaret Jones, Heather Morrey and other members of the original Pavilion Trust, as well as past and present members and officers of Rother District Council for their support, particularly Evelyn Armstrong, Ivor Brampton, Pauline Bullock, Geoff Dudman, Graham Gubby, Stephen Hardy, Brian Kentfield, Anthony Leonard, Robin Patten, David Powell, Susan Prochak, Frank Rallings, Martin Ryan, Jennie Shea and Derek Stevens. My thanks also go to the many individuals who gave their time and effort along the way, including Roger Bamber, Greg Barker, Jeremy Brook, Sir Hugh Casson, Caroline Collier, the Earl and Countess De La Warr, John Dowling, Gill Hamilton, Eddie Izzard, John Izzard, Hilary Lane, Sir Denys and Lady Susan Lasdun, Richard Morrice, Lord Palumbo, Alan Powers, Lord Rayne, Sir Nicholas Serota and Sir John Smith.

I will also take this opportunity to record my personal thanks to a number of pavilion staff who have displayed faith and hard work in getting the organization through tough times and significant change. They include Peter Caw, Vanda Curtis, Celia Davies, Jane Freund, Polly Gifford, Andrew King, Jan Lewis, Sally Ann Lycett, Bob Marsh, Emma Morris, Catherine Orbach, Blair Robinson, Natalie Trimby and Tony Williams, and those staff who have recently joined this new venture. Importantly, my thanks go to those professionals who have helped design and deliver the pavilion to a quality of which I believe Mendelsohn and Chermayeff would have been proud – in particular, architects John McAslan, Adam Brown, Umberto Emoli and Mark Cannata, engineers Tom Scholar and Peter Dunkin and project manager Nick Cragg.

The process of change could not have taken place, however, without the confidence of the artists and curators who have engaged with us over more recent times. I have been particularly honoured to have worked with Barber Osgerby, Paul Bonaventura, Colin Booth, Ian Breakwell, Jo Bruton, David Chandler, Michael Danner, Jeremy Deller, Laura Ford, Bill Gee, John Gill, Stephen Hughes, Linda Lewis, Antoni Malinowski, Daria Martin, John Riddy, The Shout, Gary Stevens, Kjell Torriset, Mark Wallinger, Boyd Webb and Richard Wilson.

My sincerest thanks go also to the Trustees of the De La Warr Pavilion Charitable Trust, including its chair, Dr Richard Sykes, and to Nikki Bell, Su Collings, Max Goodison, Orlando Gough, Joy Hughes, Penny Johnson, Ben Langlands, John Midgley, John Miller, Mark Moorton, Derek Norcross and Graham Whitham.

Finally, I offer my sincere thanks and appreciation to those who have worked on this book: to Alastair Fairley for researching and writing such enlightening text; to Bridget Smith for her subtle images of the restoration; to Richard Rogers for his inspiring foreword; to Sophia Gibb for picture research; to photographer Ian Bavington Jones, curator Julian Porter, Bexhill Museum, the *Bexhill Observer* and Bexhill Library for their help with picture research; to Orna Frommer-Dawson for her sensitive design; to Hugh Merrell, Julian Honer and all at Merrell Publishers; and lastly to Celia Davies for her sheer stamina and determination in managing this publication through to fruition.

On behalf of the De La Warr Pavilion Charitable Trust, I thank Arts Council England, Rother District Council, the Heritage Lottery Fund, English Heritage, the Headley Trust, Esmée Fairbairn Foundation, the Foyle Foundation, the Ibstock Cory Environmental Trust, Biff Awards, the Edward Marshall Trust, the Getty Foundation, the United Arab Emirates, Henry Moore Foundation, the Manifold Trust and the Mercers' Company for their capital and ongoing financial support. I also thank the many individual patrons and friends of the pavilion.

Alan Haydon, *Director of the De La Warr Pavilion*

introduction

Where the finished building strikes you as a flower which didn't exist before in the garden of architecture, where the author's original mind and specific handwriting are clearly visible – there and there alone is a creative personality, there the great architect has left his imprint for everybody to see, the literate and the illiterate, young and old. (Erich Mendelsohn, lecture delivered at the University of Los Angeles, 1948)

A remarkable building is one that stirs the imagination, an exceptional building one that excites passion. The De La Warr Pavilion at Bexhill in East Sussex succeeds in doing both. Its simple design, by Erich Mendelsohn and Serge Chermayeff, inspired architects and infuriated critics in equal measure when the building opened in 1935, yet it has withstood the ravages of war, sea and changing fashion.

This is the story of the pavilion. It is a story, not just a history. True, there is much to record: the technical innovations that so impressed architects when the pavilion was built; the building's wavering fortunes through its initial successes, then war and subsequent neglect and recent revival; and the financial cost of keeping it open, maintaining its fabric and providing the range of cultural activities staged there over the years. But the pavilion's history is also a tale of human endeavour and aspiration – the struggle to get such a novel building constructed in the first place and to open up people's minds to new ideas and new ways in which to spend their leisure time.

Today the pavilion is acknowledged as one of the finest examples of Modernist architecture anywhere in the world, a prime example of the International Style of the early twentieth century. At that period, through engineering and design innovations, building style could be, and often was, transported from one country to the next, and the shape of a building intentionally related directly to the functions to which it was being put, free from decoration, fuss or reference to a previous age. The style was new – in every sense, modern. Such ideas were not restricted only to architecture. In the aftermath of the First World War, the desire to create a new world order, free from conflict and destruction, drew leading thinkers, politicians and ideologists towards higher aspirations. Through careful planning, hard work and dedication they envisaged a more enlightened, intelligent society. Through learning could be found both enjoyment and understanding. Through innovation could be found efficiency. And with efficiency, more free time would result, liberating people's souls and helping them escape the shackles of work and focus on the good things in life.

That the De La Warr Pavilion was built at all owed much to chance. While other resorts on Britain's south coast were busy building piers, winter gardens, zoos and a host of other attractions to lure people out of London, Bexhill was procrastinating about what it should do, or whether it should do anything at all. By the time the town had decided on action, a new form of architecture was emerging, one that broke with tradition, challenged the rules and developed new techniques to achieve innovative structures. And, as Adolf Hitler started to impress his dictatorial version of the Third Reich on much of Europe, many proponents of the new architecture fled to Britain, bringing their knowledge with them. Erich Mendelsohn (1887–1953) was one of the first to arrive.

Opposite Serge Chermayeff (1900–1996) was born in Grozny, Chechnya, but was educated in England. He tried several professions before finding success as an architect and teacher.

Below Erich Mendelsohn (1887–1953) was already a renowned architect in Germany before he fled to Britain in 1933.

Below, top Structural engineer Felix Samuely (1902–1959) had already collaborated with Mendelsohn on designs in Germany when his friend enlisted his help on the pavilion in 1934.

Below, centre Architect and designer Alvar Aalto's (1898–1976) Finmar tables and chairs perfectly complemented the pavilion's contemporary interior.

Bottom Opened in 1936, William Crabtree's Peter Jones store in Chelsea, London, followed the pavilion's construction techniques.

The story of the De La Warr Pavilion, however, is not only about how it came to be built in accordance with the new ideas of the age. Lauded by architects on its opening, the pavilion itself had a major influence on the architecture of its time. Compared with the solutions conceived by other leading architects who competed for the pavilion commission, Mendelsohn and Chermayeff's design was technically outstanding. The competition was the first of its kind in the country for a Modernist building. The subsequent construction of the pavilion broke new ground, too. No one had ever seen welded steel frames used in buildings in Britain before, and the pavilion ignited a revolution in construction techniques. It was also the first project on British soil for its Austrian-born engineer, Felix Samuely, who later founded the company F.J. Samuely and Partners.

The pavilion's simple form and outline broke away from the convention of using decoration both inside and outside buildings. The interior set new standards, using colour in novel ways and incorporating soft furnishings from the most innovative manufacturers of the day. Armchairs were from PLAN, the influential modern furniture company, and the Finmar tables and seating were by the Finnish architect and designer Alvar Aalto. A huge mural was commissioned from Edward Wadsworth, today celebrated as one of the leading artists of the early twentieth century. Standard lighting was eschewed in favour of a single chrome light fitting suspended the length of the building's spiral staircase.

The pavilion's influence on other architects was immediate. Opened only one year later, in 1936, the Peter Jones department store in Chelsea, London, by William Crabtree, was built using precisely the same curtain-wall technique that Mendelsohn had adopted first in his Schocken department store buildings in Germany in the late 1920s and then used in the pavilion in Bexhill. Also in 1936, the menswear store Simpson of Piccadilly, by Joseph Emberton, likewise followed the pavilion design, not only employing a welded steel frame for its construction, but also having a similar chrome-plated light fitting running down its stairwell from top to bottom.

The pavilion introduced a new vernacular style to British seaside architecture, likened by one critic to "standing on the deck of a liner at sea". Before long, its modern lines, balustrades and banded windows were being repeated up and down the coast, from Cross and Sutton's Super Swimming Stadium in Morecambe, Lancashire (1936), and R.W.H. Jones's Saltdean Lido and Ocean Hotel, near Brighton, East Sussex (1938), to the smaller, though no less stylish 'oyster' bungalows (so called because of their shape) of Pevensey Bay, East Sussex (1937–39). Flat roofs and curving glass were now employed in abundance, and would continue to be for decades to come.

Erich Mendelsohn was no stranger to influence; indeed, before his arrival in Britain in 1933 he had been among the most influential and successful architects in Germany. Born in Allenstein, East Prussia (present-day Poland), he studied at what is now the Technical University of Berlin and subsequently in Munich. His studies, which included painting scenery and designing costumes for the theatre, brought him into contact with the exponents of the new movement of Expressionism, Paul Klee, Franz Marc and Vasily Kandinsky. The closer integration of the arts with architecture and with technology was a clear signal that a new era was emerging. But it was not until the onset of the First World War, and Mendelsohn's enlistment in the engineering corps in 1915, that his architectural thinking – and unique talent for drawing – became more fully honed. He spent the next three years on the Russian front, alternating guard duty and military offenses with quiet moments stolen away, scribbling precise, tiny sketches of fantasy buildings on what little scraps of paper he could find. Theatres, film studios, factories – Mendelsohn's art knew no bounds, but art was all it was at that time.

Mendelsohn's drawings owed much to his mentor and lifelong friend, Belgian architect Henry van de Velde. Van de Velde's focus on the line of a drawing "as a force", free from decoration, had resulted, spectacularly, in the theatre he designed for the 1914 Deutscher Werkbund exhibition in Cologne, the theatre's outline picked out by a small, continuous band of moulding highlighting its contours. By the start of the war, after his earlier, hesitant art, Mendelsohn's drawings, too, had become pure proponents of line and form. "My sketches are data, the contour lines of an instantaneous vision", he wrote to his friend and collaborator Dr Erwin Freundlich in 1917.

Van de Velde's thinking on the elastic properties of new industrial materials was also furthered by Mendelsohn's influential exhibition of wartime drawings at the Cassirer Gallery in Berlin in 1919, entitled *Architecture in Steel and Concrete*. Architecture, Mendelsohn argued, was at the dawn of a new age: with steel for support, concrete could become 'plastic' – mouldable, dynamic, the shaper of the new form. Just one year later, he was able to put this fascination with the science of architecture into practice, merging it, appropriately, with the architecture of science. By 1920 work had begun on the construction of an astrophysical observatory in Potsdam, near Berlin, intended to demonstrate Albert Einstein's theory of relativity. Based on Mendelsohn's early wartime sketches, the Einstein Tower (1921) sought to match the very latest architectural designs with novel construction techniques, all with the single goal of exploring the brave new worlds of science and technology.

The young Mendelsohn rapidly developed one of the largest architectural practices in Germany, exploring the properties of steel and concrete and applying his novel form of architecture to the buildings of the new century: factories, hospitals, cinemas. In 1924 he became joint founder of Der Ring, a group of architects whose output was characterized by dynamic, streamlined features, strip windows and new construction techniques. Mendelsohn's designs for the Schocken stores in Stuttgart (1926–27) and Chemnitz (1928) reinvented the modern department store, with reinforced concrete enabling the use of long, continuous window bands that brought light into the building by day yet transformed it into a spectacular illumination by night. The ground floor was entirely glazed; escalators carried shoppers to different floors; and air conditioning kept temperatures stable.

To many people, Mendelsohn's designs appeared more 'expressionist' than functional (an emphasis on function was one of the characteristics of the growing trend towards 'modernism'), frequently

Left The roof of Mendelsohn's Steinberg, Hermann & Co. hat factory in Luckenwalde, Germany (1921–23), incorporated industrial functions into its design.

Below, top The Schocken department store in Chemnitz, Germany (1928), looked as spectacular by day as it did by night.

Below, centre The Universum cinema (1928) gave Berlin's film-goers uninterrupted views of the screen.

stemming from his pencil fantasy sketches and owing more to personal expression than the demands of an architectural brief. Look closer, however, and the buildings' shapes and designs – their *form* – are directly linked to their function. The ground-breaking span of Mendelsohn's Universum cinema in Berlin (1928) was driven by the need for uninterrupted views of the screen, a concept universally employed today but an innovation in its time. His roof designs for the Steinberg, Hermann & Co. hat factory in Luckenwalde (1921–23) were dictated not only by aesthetics but also by the need for special ventilation to protect workers during the dyeing process. While he was regarded as a leading exponent of Expressionism, Mendelsohn was also pioneering many of the concepts central to the new Modernist style. Significantly, it had also been Mendelsohn – more than any of his contemporaries – who had made early efforts towards advancing the spread of new architectural ideas around the world. In later years Mendelsohn himself likened the De La Warr Pavilion to a "horizontal skyscraper", fulfilling his own wish for an organic relationship between building and setting, in this case the coastline. Such a concept had influenced his contemporaries years before. The American architect Frank Lloyd Wright acknowledged his German colleague and friend in the formation of his own masterly approach towards blending his buildings perfectly with their environments. Mendelsohn had stayed with Wright during an inspirational visit to the United States in 1924, holding long discussions on the meaning of architecture and the use of materials, particularly concrete and steel. As Mendelsohn had demonstrated with his Einstein Tower, he had come to see concrete as a 'plastic' material that could be shaped into many forms. Wright was clearly impressed: shortly after Mendelsohn's stay, Wright's design drawings for an automobile look-out at Sugarloaf Mountain, Maryland, used swirling, concrete roads to sweep visitors up to the peak, a technique he adapted most successfully in his final masterpiece, the Solomon R. Guggenheim Museum in New York (1959).

Other techniques pioneered by Mendelsohn, and used in the pavilion, emerged elsewhere around the world. Richard Neutra – renowned for his Modernist architecture in California – had been

Right Frank Lloyd Wright (centre) learned of Mendelsohn's (left) work when Richard Neutra (right), Mendelsohn's former assistant, worked for him in 1924.

Mendelsohn's assistant in his practice in Germany from 1921 to 1922 before leaving to work in the United States, starting his own career there with Mendelsohn's hero, Wright. Neutra adopted some of his former employer's ideas, such as the way Mendelsohn incorporated lettering on a building's façade. Just as Mendelsohn announced his pavilion in Bexhill and his department stores in Germany with a huge sign above the entrance, so the same device emerged in Neutra's own work, such as the Channel Heights Market building in San Pedro, California (1932).

Architectural ideas, like building styles, were becoming truly 'international', and Mendelsohn was at the forefront of their dissemination. During the construction of the Bexhill pavilion his contacts led him to explore opportunities in Palestine, where, through the sponsorship of the future first president of Israel, Chaim Weizmann, he carried out much of his best work, including a house in Rehovot for Weizmann himself in 1937. By 1941, however, the Second World War had caused commissions even there to dry up, leading Mendelsohn to emigrate once more, to the United States, where he finally settled in California. He died from cancer in 1953, with many designs unrealized and the early promise of his career never fully developed. Although Mendelsohn spent only a relatively brief period in America, his designs for such hospitals as the Maimonides in San Francisco (1946–50); for such private dwellings as the masterly Russell House (1950), its bay window looking out to the Golden Gate Bridge; and for synagogues and Jewish community centres; together with his lectureship in architecture at the University of California, Berkeley, are testament to the extraordinary range of his abilities.

Even at the time of his arrival in Britain in 1933, Mendelsohn was renowned as one of the great architects of his day. Such a reputation might have eclipsed the partner with whom he built the pavilion, Serge Chermayeff (1900–1996), yet Chermayeff, too, was set to exert a major influence on the architectural thinking of the twentieth century.

Born Sergei Issakovitch in Grozny, Chechnya, where his family owned an oil company, Chermayeff was sent to school in London and to Harrow, only for his family to lose their fortune in the Russian Revolution of 1917. Unable to take up his place at Cambridge University, he had an unsettled early career, working first as an illustrator for the Amalgamated Press and as a professional dancer (he won the International Tango Competition in 1927) and for two years on a ranch in Argentina. In 1924 he returned to England, where he changed his name to Sergius Chermayeff and was taken on as an interior designer by an old school friend, Ronald Trew, a partner in the firm of Ernest Williams. In 1928 he moved on to head the new Modern Art Studio and Department at Waring & Gillow, a leading London firm for interiors and furnishings.

By 1930, spurred by new thinking spreading from the Continent, Chermayeff was among a number of leading architects and designers who were exploring how design might transform English society. Their ideas led to the formation of the Twentieth Century Group, which included, among others, Wells Coates, Joseph Emberton and the young Australian architect Raymond McGrath.

In 1931 Chermayeff struck out on his own, establishing a design practice and completing successful commissions for the British Broadcasting Corporation's (BBC) new Broadcasting House, the Cambridge Theatre and his own house in Abbey Road, London. That same year, he also established PLAN, marketing modern furniture based on German models. In 1932, although he had no formal training, he successfully applied to become a Fellow of the Royal Institute of British Architects (RIBA). This award allowed him to start working on exterior designs as well as the interiors for which he had by then become well known.

Talented, handsome and successful, Chermayeff belonged to a small section of English society whose contacts, lineage and education brought both commissions and influence. The publisher Dennis Cohen, for example, was a director of PLAN; he also commissioned Chermayeff, together with Mendelsohn, to design a new home for him in Chelsea, London. Chermayeff worked with Coates and McGrath on the BBC commission. Coates had an affair with the wife of Jack Pritchard, with whom he had founded

Left The Salman Schocken residence and library in Jerusalem (1934–35) housed the rare books collection of Mendelsohn's friend and sponsor.

Below Another Mendelsohn and Chermayeff commission, Shrub's Wood (1934–35), a private house in Buckinghamshire, used terraces and glazing to bring sunlight into the heart of the living areas.

Below The Cohen House in Chelsea, London (1935–36), is one of only three Mendelsohn buildings in England.

the influential Isokon design company in 1930. Despite this, Coates, Pritchard and Chermayeff all travelled to Germany in 1931 to compile a report for *Architectural Review* that gave prominence to buildings designed by Mendelsohn, who Chermayeff had met the previous year at a lecture to launch an exhibition of his work at the Architectural Association in London. They visited him at his house, Am Rupenhorn, in Berlin, which Mendelsohn himself had designed inside and out. It was the start of a brief yet productive period for both Mendelsohn and Chermayeff.

Mendelsohn had been working on ideas for the establishment of a 'European Academy of the Mediterranean', a Bauhaus-style institute providing academic teaching and study in a variety of arts and design disciplines, drawing together ideas – and students – from all over Europe, North Africa and the Middle East. Mendelsohn asked Chermayeff to become the teacher of interior design, while Eric Gill, who had contributed sculpture and reliefs to Broadcasting House, was to be the head of typography. Although inexperienced as a teacher, Chermayeff leaped at the chance to become involved in an international scheme devised by one of Germany's leading architects, and offered his office as the London address for the academy. Ultimately, the academy never came to fruition, internal tensions (and geographical distance) leading to differences between Mendelsohn and his cofounders. But the co-operation heralded a new chapter. With Hitler's

appointment as chancellor in January 1933, work for so-called 'Bolshevik' Modernist architects had all but dried up in Germany, and persecution of Jews was rife: it was clear that Mendelsohn had to leave. Who better to turn to than his new friend and admirer, Chermayeff? Acquiring a 55 per cent stake in Chermayeff's practice, Mendelsohn brought his British partner expertise and experience. Their new practice was established in the autumn of 1933.

No sooner had Chermayeff and Mendelsohn started working together than it was announced, in 1934, that they had won the prestigious competition to design the De La Warr Pavilion, a major coup in any architect's portfolio and a huge step forward for Modernist design. The partnership was brief, spanning only three years, but Chermayeff's contacts brought two further commissions: Shrub's Wood (1934–35), a house in Chalfont St Giles, Buckinghamshire, for the oil company executive R.J. Nimmo, and a house for his friend Dennis Cohen in London's exclusive Chelsea district (1935–36).

By the time the partnership was dissolved in 1936, Chermayeff had joined the Modern Architectural Research (MARS) Group, a 'think tank' for modern British architecture founded by, among others, his friend and colleague Well Coates. Chermayeff continued to practice for a while, completing two commercial

commissions inaugurated during his partnership with Mendelsohn: the headquarters building for W. & A. Gilbey in Camden, London (1937), and a laboratory complex for ICI Dyestuffs in Blackley, Manchester (1938). Both show distinct influences from Mendelsohn, most notably the former, its façade proclaiming the name 'GILBEY' vertically in three-dimensional letters. But Chermayeff's most acclaimed work, apart from the De La Warr Pavilion, was Bentley Wood, the house he constructed for his family in Halland, East Sussex (1937–38). Timber-framed, with six squared frames on each of the two floors, the house marked Chermayeff's real break from his German mentor's influence: its design was based on zones of noise and privacy as well as visual impact, and it incorporated works from many of England's finest modern artists as key elements. Its construction also bankrupted him.

By 1940 it was time to move on. Chermayeff went to the United States, where his experience in architectural theory led him to start a new career in teaching rather than practising architecture. In 1947 he became the director of the Institute of Design in Chicago after the death of its founder, the former Bauhaus teacher László Moholy-Nagy (who, coincidentally, had taken a famous series of photographs of the De La Warr Pavilion for *The Architects' Journal* shortly after its opening).

From Chicago, Chermayeff went, in 1951, to Cambridge, Massachusetts, as a visiting lecturer at the Massachusetts Institute of Technology (MIT), then in 1953 to Harvard, where he took up the post of professor of architecture. Nine years later, he moved to Yale, where he taught (among many others) two young men now renowned as the principal architects of their generation, Richard Rogers and Norman Foster. Chermayeff's book *Community and Privacy* (1963), on the dynamics of designing for the modern age, so influenced the pair that they modelled the first housing project by their short-lived Team 4 architectural practice – working for the builder and developer Wates on a site in Croydon, Surrey (1964–65) – on his concepts. Rogers, in particular, still credits his former teacher's influence on his work as chief adviser to the British government on urban regeneration.

Left A photograph taken at the opening of the MARS Group Exhibition in January 1938 shows, from left to right: Godfrey Samuel, Le Corbusier, Wells Coates, J.M. Richards, Serge Chermayeff and Maxwell Fry.

Clearly, then, the De La Warr Pavilion was conceived by architectural visionaries, but the man whose name the building now bears was just as pivotal in its development. Herbrand Edward Dundonald Brassey Sackville (1900–1976), the 9th Earl De La Warr, was a rare individual: a wealthy aristocrat whose title had existed for centuries, and yet whose unconventional upbringing and close relationship with leading thinkers of the time fuelled a deep concern for the plight of his fellow man.

De La Warr's hand can be seen in several later events in British history. He was one of only a few cabinet ministers to persuade the prime minister, Neville Chamberlain, of the necessity of declaring war on Germany in 1939. That same year, as president of the Board of Education, his idea for a post-war Thames-side celebration of the arts found support in Lord Macmillan, then minister of information and responsible for national morale. De La Warr's proposal eventually led to the establishment of the wartime Council for the Encouragement of Music and the Arts – the fore-runner of today's Arts Council – and, ultimately, the 1951 Festival of Britain, which, as De La Warr had hoped, played a valuable role in providing artistic refreshment to a war-shattered Britain. Returning to cabinet office as postmaster-general in Winston Churchill's 1951 government, De La Warr oversaw a string of ground-breaking developments, including the launch of the international telex service, the planning of the national telephone numbering scheme and the laying of the transatlantic telephone cable, and in 1954 he pioneered the bill through parliament to establish independent television in the United Kingdom.

The story of the De La Warr Pavilion, however, also captures many of the events of the last century within its frame. The pavilion's wartime record bears scars from many of the same incidents that befell the inhabitants of the town in which the building stands. The determination of those inhabitants meant that, bombed and battered, the pavilion kept its doors open to lift the spirits of thousands who sought some light relief during the conflict. It was to the pavilion that they came in the celebratory atmosphere of the post-war period, when people could once more enjoy holidays at the seaside. And, as the constant drum of 'progress' saw holidaymakers travel to other, foreign destinations, so the decline of the pavilion's fortunes paralleled the nation's general descent into recession and unemployment.

By the same token, the pavilion's recent resurgence adds yet another commentary – this time on the nation's urban renaissance and its new approach towards the built environment. Indeed, the raising by the Pavilion Trust of the issue of the pavilion's plight as a historic monument under severe threat not only saved it from the bulldozer and, later, developer; it likewise brought the matter to the attention of the authorities. Their response, in the form of funds

Below Earl De La Warr's vision of a Thames-side festival was finally realized with the opening of the Festival of Britain in 1951.

from the National Lottery, offered a financial lifeline not only to the pavilion but also to scores of other buildings throughout the country. That this remarkable building should have played its part – no matter how small – in the resurgence of Britain as a world centre for culture is testament to its power to move people who know it and have come to love it. Today the arts and culture are increasingly seen as foundation stones in the regeneration of decaying towns and cities, a process that the De La Warr Pavilion is leading in Bexhill and across the south-east region in general.

It is also entirely appropriate that the building's restoration and redevelopment, now complete, have been conducted by the leading architectural firm John McAslan + Partners, whose remodelling of Charles Rennie Mackintosh's 78 Derngate in Northampton (1916), Crabtree's Peter Jones store in Chelsea and Wright's Florida Southern College, Lakeland (1938–58), as well as Mendelsohn's Einstein Tower and Steinberg, Hermann & Co. hat factory has retraced the footsteps of Modern Movement pioneers around the world.

Today, once more, the De La Warr Pavilion seeks to be a centre not only for the people of Bexhill but also for visitors across the region, the country and from around the world. Lovers of architecture, families, passers-by seeking refuge from the chill east wind – all are welcome in this new, exciting venture.

In the early 1880s Bexhill was little more than a country village in eastern Sussex, on the English Channel coast. Its inhabitants, who numbered around two thousand at that time, could reach the shingle beach over streams and along the cliffs, an hour's walk from the Victorian towns of Hastings and St Leonards, or a half-day journey by horse and carriage from the Georgian splendour of Brighton, with its new piers and royal patronage.

Yet the building of Bexhill's finest cultural asset, the De La Warr Pavilion, some fifty years later, was more than the result of a town seeking to improve itself and compete with its neighbours. Spurred on by the succession of wealthy and active patrons and a progressive town council, the development of Bexhill and the construction of its pavilion is a tale in which many of the events, fashions and social trends of the late nineteenth and early twentieth centuries are mapped out.

The Industrial Revolution was already driving the development of the British seaside coast long before the 7th Earl De La Warr (1817–1896) set about building on the land he owned in Bexhill to make the town a fashionable seaside resort. With money and leisure time for the first time, Britain's new working classes flocked to the country's coastlines every summer throughout the Victorian era to escape the smoke of the towns and cities.

Large seaside resorts started to develop and expand, including Margate, Blackpool and Brighton. Towers and winter gardens sprang up, along with entertainments devised to amuse the crowds: music halls, variety and dancing, zoos, aquariums, theatres and exhibition halls. As seaside towns grew during the Victorian era, the pier became the focus of the resort; between 1862 and 1872 eighteen new piers were built. These 'pleasure' piers included amusement halls and theatres to entertain the visiting crowds. Growth was rapid: by 1888 Eastbourne had built a 400-seat pavilion dome on its pier, replacing it just eleven years later with a 1000-seat theatre and camera obscura to cater for the increasing numbers of tourists.

The 7th Earl De La Warr was keen to capitalize on the tourist trade. He was already a wealthy man: when he began the construction of his new seaside resort, it was allegedly possible to walk from London to the south coast without leaving De La Warr land. In 1883 he constructed Bexhill's sea wall, enabling elegant parades of houses and shops to be built, and added 'on Sea' to the town's name. It was a clear message that Bexhill, with its new railway link to London, had arrived as a coastal resort.

The earl's son, Gilbert Sackville (1869–1915), the flamboyant Viscount Cantelupe, continued the process yet further. Assuming control of the estate from his father in 1892, the 8th Earl began creating Bexhill's 'golden age', building at a furious pace and, with his remarkable wife, Muriel, setting the tone of the town. The 7th Earl had wanted to distinguish Bexhill from its neighbours, as did his son and grandson after him. In the early 1890s, for example, he had banned various types of entertainer from performing on land he owned on the seafront in order to discourage rowdy behaviour, which he felt

Above The 7th Earl De La Warr (1817–1896) developed Bexhill as a fashionable seaside resort.

Below, top While other seaside resorts thrived at the beginning of the twentieth century, Bexhill had only its beaches to offer.

Below, centre Brighton's West Pier had been a fashionable attraction for thousands of visitors since 1866.

Bottom Between 1918 and 1935 Hastings, pictured here in 1904, invested £3,500,000 in its promenade.

Above Blackpool's beaches provided escape from the smog and grime of the city.

Below, top In 1895 Bexhill became the first British resort to allow mixed-sex bathing, a bold move to distinguish it from other resorts.

Below, centre Bexhill's original entertainments pavilion, the Kursaal, was one of the first in the country to show motion pictures.

Bottom The Kursaal was but one feature of the town's grand Edwardian promenade, where fashionable crowds took the sea air.

was inappropriate to the atmosphere he had sought to create. It was a principle his son aimed to uphold. All the main hotels were built in this period, the Metropole (1900) and the Granville (1902) being the grandest, and two golf clubs were constructed. In 1896 the 8th Earl built the Kursaal Pavilion to provide high-class entertainment for the resort. Housing, hotels, even entertainment were all designed to attract the wealthier and more 'respectable' type of person, but also had a modern dimension.

Perhaps in a bid to distinguish itself from the equally respectable yet rather sedate Eastbourne, the town of Bexhill also adopted an innovatory approach. In 1895 it became the first British resort to permit mixed-sex bathing. A cycle track was laid along the East Parade, and international cycling tournaments were held, including one in 1897 attended by Grand Duke Michael of Russia. In 1898 the Kursaal became one of the first places in the country to show motion pictures. Perhaps most startling of all, in 1902 Bexhill's seafront became the first place in Britain to host motor races. The 8th Earl had been quick to spot the headlines such events might produce when, in his role as chairman of the Dunlop Tyre company, he witnessed the world's first such races on a visit to Nice in 1901.

By the turn of the twentieth century, then, the foundations had been laid for Bexhill's transformation into an upmarket seaside resort for the fashionable, well-heeled society that the 7th and 8th Earls wanted to attract. But it had cost a great deal of money. Not only had Bexhill's development nearly bankrupted the 8th Earl, but much of the initial building work had been completed only through a deal his father had struck with a local contractor, John Webb, who received a large portion of the town's land in return for carrying out the work involved. The divisions the deal created were to beset the town – and the fortunes of the pavilion for which it is now famous – for much of the following century. As the two earls had clearly set out to achieve, Bexhill did not offer the dogs and horse races of Brighton, or the cheap and cheerful attractions of nearby Hastings. The resort rapidly became known as a residential town by the sea, where respectable people of independent means could live and enjoy their leisure time. But,

Below By the 1930s the seaside towns of Sussex were jointly promoting the 'Conqueror's Coast'.

as former resident Evelyn Older explained in the 1970s, this had major consequences for the people who lived and worked there: "Bexhill was a very divided place. Three-quarters worked as servants, gardeners, boot-boys. Dorset Road, Cantelupe Road, all those houses were occupied by one family with not less than three servants. That side, that's where all the work was" (Gray 1994, p. 19).

In contrast to the wealthy residences, grand hotels and high-class entertainment attractions on De La Warr land, John Webb's estate, now known as Egerton Park, was home to tradesmen, shops and services. While neither one could exist without the other, the two sets of Bexhill residents never mixed socially. The divisions went beyond geographical location or the resulting snobbery, however. At their heart lay the divide between those who depended on tourism, and those wealthier residents who saw any tourists – high-class or not – as intrusions on their quiet, respectable lives. When it came to deciding who was going to pay for facilities to attract the tourists, differing opinions provoked strident argument. For example, in 1895 the future 8th Earl, increasingly short of money, attempted to sell much of the seafront land he owned to the town's municipal authority. When it refused to meet his asking price he responded by erecting gates to the estate, symbolically cutting the seafront in two. This led to his direct involvement in the provision of town entertainments: the following year he commissioned the construction of the Kursaal Pavilion for "refined entertainment and relaxation".

In 1907 various proposals were put forward for the development of a 'winter garden' in order to attract year-round visitors, culminating in 1911 in the opening of the Colonnade bandstand, the principal rotundas of which still stand in front of the De La Warr Pavilion. Even this move was controversial, however, with the local newspaper, the *Bexhill-on-Sea Observer* printing cartoons of angry musical battles between the Colonnade and Kursaal bands driving away the town's tourist lifeblood as they vied for supremacy. As 'H.M.' of the *Methodist Recorder* later noted: "I remember the controversy when it was proposed to build a new Colonnade, and the little colony of fashionable retired folk, who strolled on the front at night in evening dress, began to complain that their favourite resort would become noisy and 'trippery' and went in search of newer places" (9 January 1936). Only when the town finally succeeded in acquiring the earl's De La Warr Parade in 1913 did the argument subside, and then only for a brief period. Having united much of the seafront in public ownership for the first time, one of the first steps that Bexhill Corporation took was to tear down the De La Warr gates the 8th Earl had erected just eighteen years before.

Other forces were also at play in determining Bexhill's fortunes as a playground for the well-to-do. With the younger generation decimated by the First World War, Britain's economy after 1918 was slow to recuperate. Deserting the south coast, the country's wealthy increasingly sought refuge in the newly fashionable resorts of the Continent, with Biarritz and the Mediterranean resorts becoming more popular. Aware of the situation, the British government introduced legislation in 1923 that paved the way for the second major phase of municipal development of the coast, allowing local councils far greater autonomy than ever before in spending on public buildings for entertainment.

Pages 26–27 The 8th Earl De La Warr staged the first-ever motor races in England on Bexhill seafront in 1902.

In an effort to regain their status, Sussex seaside towns started to invest heavily in new attractions to lure their former visitors back to British shores. Between 1918 and 1935 Hastings and St Leonards spent £3,500,000 on a series of improvements, including swimming pools, theatres, bowling greens and underground car parks.

Bexhill also embarked on a programme of development. In 1926 the corporation commissioned the architects Adams, Thomson & Fry to produce a development plan for the town, ostensibly to control the growth of residential building on the town's outskirts. However, the final report, produced in 1930, concluded that the future prosperity of Bexhill depended largely on the improvement of conditions in the town's central area. The success of other neighbouring towns in attracting visitors had not escaped the planners' notice. The growing trend for music festivals, and the securing of prestigious conductors, singers and soloists in such places as the Bournemouth Winter Gardens, home to the municipal orchestra, demonstrated how effectively the arts could generate revenue. As a result, featured in the Bexhill borough 'General Development Plan' was a series of proposed buildings, illustrated by one of the architects' partners, Maxwell Fry. Principal among these was a 'Music Pavilion and Enlarged Band Enclosure', which the plan suggested should be located on the site of the coastguard station, destined for closure that year. It was to be the genesis of the De La Warr Pavilion.

To combat further the flow of seaside tourism to the new resorts of France and elsewhere on the Continent, the coastal towns of Sussex joined together in 1930 to promote the 'Conqueror's Coast' (ironically, a reference to their Norman foundation), collaborating on marketing and other ventures to win back the English tourists. The obstacles were considerable. The General Strike of 1926 had been a foretaste of the economic troubles that were unleashed by the Wall Street Crash of 1929. Money, especially the spare cash to spend on holidays, was tight. However, in 1931, after six years of struggling to compete internationally by adhering to the gold standard monetary system, the new government finally succumbed to pressure, devalued the currency and left the standard for good. For the coastal resorts this was good news. Finally, foreign travel was to become considerably more expensive than its English alternative, and the visitors started to return.

The railways also contributed to the recovery, with the Southern Railway opening a network of new, electrified routes in July 1935 at a cost of £1,750,000. Under pressure from the towns of the Conqueror's Coast, the London, Midland & Scottish Railway Company also agreed to provide routes to the Channel direct from the Midlands and the North, bypassing London and bringing many new tourists to Sussex on its Sunny South Express train. As advertising campaigns promoted the region's climate, its facilities and its particular brand of the 1930s idyll to new visitors, so the

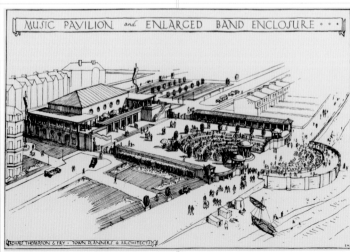

'Wealth of Health' coast also developed a retirement belt. Popular new bungalows cost as little as £450, and their single-storey construction and small patch of garden appealed to a large number of retired people.

It was towards Bexhill, with its genteel atmosphere and attractions, that this new migration headed. Alone among the southern coastal resorts, Bexhill's population grew by 4 per cent between 1921 and 1931, rising to 21,229. The neighbouring resorts stagnated or declined: the population of Brighton remained static in the same period, while the populations of Hastings and Eastbourne fell by 2 per cent and 7 per cent respectively. By contrast, in the twenty years from 1900 to 1920, the population of Bexhill had grown by an average of 30 per cent, a much faster rate than the populations of its neighbours. For the first thirty years of the twentieth century Bexhill was the boomtown of the East Sussex coast.

Although Bexhill's rapidly growing residential population meant that the town was less dependent on seasonal tourism for its economic fortunes, it failed to quell the old disputes over who was to pay for the town's future attractions, as proposed in the borough's development plan. Indeed, the residents' differing views made matters worse. Taking up the development baton in 1930, the mayor, Councillor A. Turner Laing, commissioned the architectural firm of Tubbs & Messer to outline a £50,000 scheme for an entertainments hall for the coastguard site identified by Adams, Thomson & Fry in its report of that year. It was to include a museum and a library and reading room, as well as facilities for music and other forms of entertainment on the Colonnade.

Keen to encourage tourism, the town's shopkeepers and hoteliers all supported the scheme, but they found themselves in dispute with the growing number of retired residents who wanted to keep Bexhill the quiet, select place they preferred. Forming a highly vocal ratepayers' association, this conservative band sought to block any attempts to expand the town to compete with such rival tourist resorts as Hastings, Brighton and Margate. As debate raged in the council chamber the impasse lasted for two more

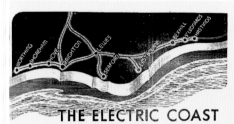

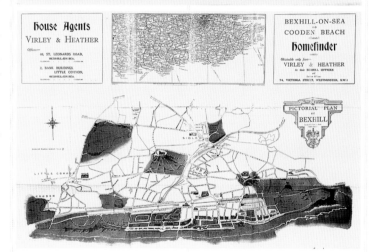

Top New, electric trains bypassed London, bringing visitors direct to the south coast from the Midlands.

Above Bexhill's sunny location and genteel atmosphere made it a popular place for retirement.

years, prompting one former mayor, Alderman Bending, to compare the situation to "a number of doctors standing around a patient's bed arguing as to the best means of curing him but, failing to agree as to a remedy, allowing the patient to continue to suffer and even get worse" (*Bexhill-on-Sea Observer*, 27 May 1933, p. 3).

While the views of Bexhill's residents changed little, in the rest of the country times were moving on. Prosperity began to return to the nation during the 1930s. Increasing industrialization meant that people had more leisure time, and the economic opportunities offered by tourism were increasingly hard to dismiss, particularly for a town in the middle of a seaside tourism boom. Politically, too, the atmosphere was changing: the new creeds of socialism, such as the placing of decision-making in the hands of communities, were on the rise both in Britain and on the Continent.

The impact of socialism was soon to appear in conservative Bexhill, too, in the shape of the new young mayor, the 9th Earl De La Warr, who was elected in 1932. Smart, quick-witted and wealthy, 'Buck' De La Warr, as he was known, was already a junior minister for agriculture and a leading force in the new National Labour Party, of which he was chairman. His father and grandfather had built much of the town, so he was acquainted with the disputes that had dominated local politics.

For a brief period, this seaside town became the focus of an extraordinary example of socialism in action, centred on the creation of an entertainments pavilion that, ultimately, was to bear the name of the man who brought it into being, Earl De La Warr. Few people could have predicted the impact the building would have on the town or on architectural and town-planning practice.

Right The new fashion for bungalows lured retirees to the south coast in their droves.

The Right Hon. Earl De La Warr, Mayor of Bexhill 1933-1934-1935.

Above Dashing, rich and talented, the socialist 9th Earl
De La Warr (1900–1976) transformed Bexhill.

chapter 2   the competition for the de la warr pavilion

While the town of Bexhill had been mulling over how to make its mark in the nation's increasingly competitive array of seaside attractions, a new style of architecture had been emerging on the Continent. Designs for factories, schools and housing were relating far more closely to their function; versatile materials such as concrete and steel were enabling the creation of new shapes; and decoration was giving way to uniform planes. Shape, form and function were the modern architect's new bywords.

By the time Bexhill announced the competition to design its new entertainments pavilion in September 1933, the new architectural ideas had started to spread across the English Channel. Amyas Connell's High and Over house in Amersham, Buckinghamshire (1929–31), had used concrete as a key part of its construction. Joseph Emberton's Royal Corinthian Yacht Club in Burnham-on-Crouch, Essex (1930–31), had showed a lightness of construction that broke the mould of heavy English stone or brickwork. Sir E. Owen Williams's Boots Packed Wet Goods Factory at Beeston, Nottinghamshire (1930–32), had an internal frame of reinforced concrete columns supporting huge concrete floor-slabs, enabling the external walls, which were not load-bearing, to be glazed from floor to ceiling, not unlike Erich Mendelsohn's eventual design for the pavilion.

The new architecture was concerned not only with the form of buildings, however, but also with the entire fabric of society, socially, economically and politically. If buildings were to be designed as "machines for living", as Le Corbusier argued, why not towns and cities? Groups such as the Congrès internationaux d'architecture moderne (CIAM), which Le Corbusier founded, or schools such as the Bauhaus (founded in 1919 by Mendelsohn's friend and colleague Walter Gropius) argued that, if development was to be planned and architects were to be the planners, architecture in the future inevitably also required political vision and power. This perceived threat gave rise to the persecution of the new breed of modern architect by the Nazis during their rise to power in Germany in the 1930s. The new ideas associated with Modernism were likened to Bolshevism; they were regarded as revolutionary, socialist, threatening and, largely owing to the fact that many of Modernism's proponents also happened to be Jewish, Zionist. The day after Hitler's assumption of control of the German parliament, the Reichstag, on 23 March 1933, Mendelsohn became the first of many architects to flee his native land, arriving in Britain in June 1933. In subsequent years he was followed by such luminaries as Gropius and Marcel Breuer. Britain, with its fledgling Modernist architectural movement, became recognized as the world centre of cutting-edge design.

Right Amyas Connell's design for the private house High and Over, in Amersham, Buckinghamshire (1929–31), used smooth render instead of heavy exposed brickwork.

As Mendelsohn's first commission in his new country, the De La Warr Pavilion was at the forefront of the new trend. With its brief to aim for simplicity of design and lightness of appearance, and offering an opportunity to use new construction techniques, Bexhill's competition to design and build the pavilion was, in effect, the first of its kind in Britain in which a 'modern' design was sought. Reaching that point was a tortuous process for this conventional seaside resort.

Had the local politicians not disagreed for so long over who was to build and pay for a new entertainments attraction for the town, Bexhill would today only rank alongside other seaside resorts with a crumbling Edwardian pier or a traditional winter garden. Adams, Thomson & Fry's report to Bexhill Corporation, delivered, with its design proposals, as early as 1930, had already suggested that the town's future prosperity depended on improving conditions and facilities in its centre. The town lagged behind other resorts that had invested in attracting tourists, such as Worthing, where a Regency-style pavilion, designed by the firm of Adshead & Ramsey, had been built in 1926. Only in 1933, through the intervention of Bexhill's new mayor, the 9th Earl De La Warr, was the impasse broken. In both politics and architecture, the time was ripe for new thinking.

Left Hitler's Third Reich offered no quarter for Germany's independent-thinking, and often Jewish, architects.

Top left Walter Gropius (left) soon followed his friend Mendelsohn (right) to Britain from Nazi Germany.

Below The pavilion was to be built on a site
(indicated on the map) formerly occupied
by the town's coastguard station.

Below The young earl had become accustomed to public
duties, even as a boy. In 1908 he laid the commemoration
stone for the extension to Bexhill's town hall.

De La Warr was committed to creating a new order in society and, like many of his contemporaries, was confident that such a new order could be brought about. 'Buck' De La Warr was not a conventional politician. Born in 1900 into a family with power and wealth, he became one of the leading lights of socialism in 1930s Britain. Responsibility was thrust on him at an early age. The then Lord Buckhurst was only two when his parents divorced. On his father's death in 1915 Buck succeeded to the earldom, presenting himself to parliament for the first time in 1918. Rejecting the ermine and velvet of his forebears, the young earl donned instead his able seaman's uniform, which he had worn during his time in the Navy in the First World War. Shortly after, on taking up his seat, he became the first hereditary peer to represent the newly formed Labour Party in the House of Lords. By 1924 he was a government whip and lord-in-waiting to the king.

Although title, position and ancestry may have brought with them certain duties for the young earl, it is the influence of Buck's mother, Muriel, that can be seen as the foundation for his approach towards carrying them out. A leading campaigner for women's suffrage and trade union rights, she came from a successful but unconventional family. Her grandfather Thomas Brassey made a fortune from building railways; King George V ennobled her father as Earl Brassey in return for his work first as member of parliament for Hastings and then as Civil Lord of the Admiralty and governor

of Victoria in Australia. But her mother, Annie, one of the first pioneering women travellers, was equally capable, and her diaries of her voyages across the world's oceans in the family yacht, *The Sunbeam*, became a bestselling book. Mixing politics with high office, adventure with civic responsibility, the family had a profound impact on the young earl.

In Buck De La Warr, therefore, Bexhill had an unusual new mayor. Already a junior minister for agriculture and chairman of Ramsay MacDonald's new National Labour Party, De La Warr had wide-ranging experience. His long-term family connections with the town (where he still owned substantial tracts) enabled him to gain the support of the public, even though his left-leaning politics seemed at odds with the conservatism that had characterized the place for years. His background was to prove invaluable: the pavilion project called on all his connections and faculties. Following his installation as mayor, De La Warr immediately set to work on the proposed pavilion project, delicately balancing the politics of the town with a series of public meetings about the new building and finally gaining overwhelming support for the proposals. The debate focused on whether the project should be financed privately or supported by public funds. The issue was so significant that a ratepayers' association was formed to take forward the debate. In May 1933, at a public meeting at the town hall held by the association, the socialist mayor came out fighting:

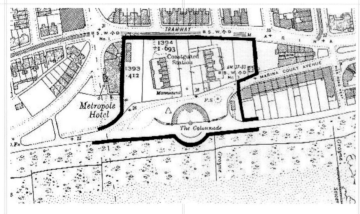

the Corporation, which will be appropriated for housing purposes, or on cleared sites acquired under compulsory purchase orders. Three types are proposed. There will be 1,750 at £365 each, 2,750 at £380 each, and 500 at £440 each, and the total cost for houses will be £1,903,750.

The remainder of the scheme provides for tenements for the inner areas, on sites to be cleared and purchased under compulsory orders, and adjacent sites. The total proposed under the new ten-year scheme is 10,692 tenements.

BRITISH INDUSTRIES FAIR

Although the British Industries Fair does not open until February 19, the Department of Overseas Trade reports that it has already received applications for more than 90 per cent. of the space occupied by exhibitors at Olympia and in the Furniture Section at the White City at the last Fair. In the "heavy industries" section, at Birmingham, advance bookings of space by exhibitors are so far ahead of those last year, or indeed, in any previous year, that some 55,000 square feet of indoor area are being added immediately to meet pressing demands.

ARCHITECTURAL CONTROL IN THE PEAK DISTRICT

The architectural panel in the Peak District has recently agreed to advise on a proposed housing scheme at Hope that is to be carried out by a firm of cement manufacturers. The original designs were considered to be unsatisfactory, and both layout and elevations were redrafted. The new drawings were accepted without demur. This is a typical example of the work which an architectural panel can accomplish in cases where there was no possibility of an architect being employed.

NEWS CINEMA FOR LIVERPOOL

The Liverpool magistrates have approved plans for a "news" cinema, which is to be built in Williamson Street, Liverpool. The approval was given on the understanding that "there must be no queues and no waiting in the foyer."

EXHIBITIONS

Today, at 3 o'clock, Sir William Crawford, K.B.E., will open an exhibition of modern industrial photography at the Royal Institute (Princes) Galleries, Piccadilly, W.

The seventy-eighth annual international exhibition of the Royal Photographic Society will be held at the Society's Galleries, 35 Russell Square, W.C.1, from Saturday, September 9, to Saturday, October 7. The Exhibition will be open daily (Sundays excepted) from 10 a.m. to 9 p.m., except on Tuesdays and Fridays, when it will close at 6 p.m. Lectures will be given on those evenings.

PUBLIC LIGHTING CONFERENCE

The tenth annual conference of the Association of Public Lighting Engineers was held at Margate from September 4-6.

On Monday last the delegates were entertained by the Mayor of Margate (Ald. F. L. Pettman, J.P.) and the Mayoress, and on the following day the Mayor opened the Conference. Following an address by the President, Mr. E. M. Severn (London), Mr. A. V. Emptage, Public Lighting Superintendent of Margate, described the lighting of the town and Mr. W. N. C. Clinch, Brighton's electrical engineer, read a paper on "The Lighting of Seaside and Health Resorts."

On Tuesday a paper was read by Mr. G. H. Wilson on "Electric discharge lamps and their applications to Public Lighting."

On Wednesday (yesterday) the following papers were read: "Street Lighting in the Irish Free State," by Mr. F. X. Algar; "Public Lighting of Paris," by Mr. J. W. Partridge (Chief Engineer in charge of street lighting, Paris); and "Public Lighting of Bombay," by Mr. J. P. Blackmore.

CHANGE OF ADDRESS

Mr. A. O. Chatterley, B.ARCH., A.R.I.B.A., has changed his Birmingham business address to 41 Water Street, Birmingham, 3. Telephone No: Central 8184.

ARCHITECT'S WILL

Mr. C. Kempson, F.R.I.B.A., of Leicester, left £19,641 (net personalty £17,457).

COMPETITION

NEWS

BEXHILL ENTERTAINMENTS HALL

It is announced this week that conditions for the above competition are now obtainable. For details see *Competitions Open* below.

Competitions Open

September 11.—Sending-in Day. The Directors of Gidea Park, Ltd., invite designs for five different types of house (ranging from £400 to £900). Assessors: Prof. S. D. Adshead, F.R.I.B.A., A. E. Beresford, F.R.I.B.A., Ald. Ewart G. Culpin, F.R.I.B.A., E. Maxwell Fry, A.R.I.B.A., Howard Robertson, F.R.I.B.A., and W. Harding Thompson, F.R.I.B.A. In addition to being paid a fee according to the scale of charges of the R.I.B.A., the authors of the first five selected designs in each class will be paid a premium of £10. Particulars obtainable from Gidea Park, Ltd., The Estate Office, Hare Street, Gidea Park, Romford, Essex. Deposit 5s.

September 21.—Sending-in Day. Proposed Town Hall for the Borough of Hornsey.

Assessor: C. Cowles-Voysey, F.R.I.B.A. Premiums: £350, £250 and £150. Full conditions, etc., were published in our issue for May 17.

September 30.—Competition for speculative house designs, organized by the Architectural Association with the co-operation of Messrs. J. Laing and Sons, Ltd. Three types of house are required. Assessors: C. Lovett Gill, F.R.I.B.A.; L. H. Bucknell, F.R.I.B.A.; J. R. Leathart, F.R.I.B.A.; Arthur W. Kenyon, F.R.I.B.A.; T. Alwyn Lloyd, F.R.I.B.A.; and J. W. Laing. Premiums: £25 for the design placed first in each group. Copies of the conditions are being issued free, on application, to all members of the Architectural Association, and members of the R.I.B.A. can obtain copies (price 2s. 6d.) from Mr. F. R. Yerbury, General Secretary, The Architectural Association, 34-36, Bedford Square, W.C.1. Full particulars of the competition were published in *A.J.* for July 27.

December 4.—Sending-in Day. Proposed Entertainments Hall, etc., for the Borough of Bexhill. Assessor: Thomas S. Tait, F.R.I.B.A. Premiums: £150, £100 and £75. Conditions, etc., obtainable from Mr. S. J. Taylor, Town Clerk, Town Hall, Bexhill-on-Sea. Deposit £1.

Competitions Pending

Proposed New Council Offices to be erected at Salt Hill for the Slough U.D.C. Assessor: H. S. Goodhart-Rendel, F.R.I.B.A. Premiums: £150, £100 and £50. Conditions have not yet been drawn up.

Proposed extensions to the Town Hall, Swindon. Assessor: Professor A. B. Knapp-Fisher, F.R.I.B.A. Conditions have not yet been drawn up.

Proposed Municipal Sanatorium and Craymount Children's Hospital, Belfast. Limited to architects practising in Northern Ireland. Assessor: R. S. Wilshere A.R.I.B.A. Conditions are now being drawn up by the assessor.

Decoration of a café-restaurant. Assessors: G. Grey Wornum, F.R.I.B.A.; Louis de Soissons, F.R.I.B.A.; and G. Alan Fortescue, F.R.I.B.A. Premiums: 50 guineas, 15 guineas and 10 guineas. Conditions governing the competition, which closes on December 15, 1933, will be issued on September 30 next.

Proposed town hall and municipal buildings, Stoke Newington. Assessor: Sir Edwin Lutyens, R.A. Conditions have not yet been drawn up.

THIS ARSHETECTURE

We have done our utmost to prevent the new Battersea Power Station being a blot on the landscape. And in building a power station which is architecturally dignified and ornamental, we have also endeavoured to combine, as far as possible, every known economy.

He (Sir Francis) also spoke of the architectural features of the station, and of an attractiveness perhaps unlooked for until one remembers that the architect of the building is Sir Gilbert Scott.

[*From an interview with Sir Francis Fladgate, the Chairman of the London Power Company, published in* THE OBSERVER *for August 27.*]

Page 35 The original announcement of
the competition appeared in *The Architects'
Journal* in September 1933 (see third column).

"My own view is," he said, "if it is going to pay private enterprise it is going to pay the town." His arguments for public funds to cover the cost were so persuasive that the proposal was agreed, with only one hand raised in opposition.

That the mayor had a strategy for securing the pavilion's future is, with hindsight, clear to see. With public support for the idea now established, the pavilion's form was to be the next challenge. De La Warr declared at the ratepayers' meeting that "We don't want this small, select town of ours to go in for a great scheme of development and attempt to compete with Hastings, Eastbourne and Brighton. ... A great number of our visitors come here because we are different." Few could have imagined just how different De La Warr's vision was to be.

Now able to proceed, yet still wary of critics, De La Warr announced that the council would hold an open competition for the building's design. He wrote to the president of the RIBA, Sir Raymond Unwin, asking him to nominate an assessor for the competition who might be "in touch with modern ideas of architectural development". Unwin's recommendation was Thomas S. Tait, whose work as a partner in the firm of Burnet, Tait & Lorne brought acceptance for him among the older generation of architects, yet whose more recent work, particularly in such projects as the Silver End housing estate in Braintree, Essex (1927), had shown leanings towards Modernist ideas.

De La Warr's own views on design are not chronicled, but that he was a Modernist, in principle, there seems little doubt. His circle of friends, among them the shipping heiress Emerald Cunard and the art collector Ivor Churchill, included the intelligentsia of Britain. And as the Nazis sought to portray Modernist architecture – and architects – as Bolshevik and Semitic, Modernism and the architecture it promoted became both fashionable among and synonymous with left-wing politicians, who had De La Warr at their heart. It is likely, therefore, that the design brief of the competition announced in *The Architects' Journal* on 7 September 1933 was prepared by Thomas Tait with input from Earl De La Warr.

The cost of the building was to be £50,000, although the council raised this limit by another £10,000 a month later. Entries had to be anonymous, and premiums of £150, £100 and £75 were offered to the first-, second- and third-placed entries. However, while the conditions gave a great deal of freedom to entrants, some of the guidelines suggested that a Modernist solution would be preferred. The main features of the pavilion were to be:

An Entertainments Hall to seat 1500 persons, to be used for concerts, theatrical performances, lectures, etc.

An Entrance Hall giving access to all public rooms.

A Restaurant (available for dancing if necessary) to seat 200 persons, designed as a sun parlour with sliding or opening French windows leading on to a terrace facing the sea.

A Conference Hall to seat 200 persons which could also be used as a lecture hall.

A Reading Room for newspapers and magazines, again in the form of a sun parlour.

A Lounge, adjacent to the reading room.

The clues were in the detail. Together with the brief and the site plan, each of the competitors received information on the kind of building the council had in mind to develop: "No restrictions as to style of architecture will be imposed, but buildings must be simple, light in appearance and attractive, suitable for a holiday resort. Heavy stonework is not desirable."

The finish was left to the discretion of competitors, "but, if cement, must not craze". Character could be added to the building's design through the use of large window spaces, terraces and canopies, and the roofs of the restaurant and reading room were also to function as "sitting-out terraces". Furthermore, "modern steel-framed or ferro-cement construction" could be adopted, with window frames to be either in wood or gun-metal. Although not explicit in the instructions, anything more descriptive of a building of the Modernist style would be hard to imagine.

The competition was set to close on 4 December. Over the following months, issues of both *The Architects' Journal* and *Architect and Building News* carried reviews of what was rapidly becoming one of the most talked-about competitions in recent years. *The Architects' Journal*, in particular, enthused over the opportunity the pavilion offered, pointing out that "with Mr Tait as assessor, [British architects] need fear no bias in favour of Victorian or any other tradition, but can strike out individually and boldly for whatever conception of modern styles their imagination dictates" (vol. 78, 28 September 1933, p. 380). The journalists were not wrong about the competition's appeal: when it finally closed on 29 December, extended to cover the Christmas break, it had attracted 230 entries.

Over the following month, Tait worked furiously to scrutinize the entries, announcing the results in *The Architects' Journal* at the beginning of February 1934. One entry had stood out above all others: the design by the new practice of Erich Mendelsohn and Serge Chermayeff.

First (£150):
Erich Mendelsohn and Serge Chermayeff, FRIBA

Second (£100):
J.W. Haswell and George H. Shepherd, A/ARIBA

Third (£75):
Philip G. Freeman and William F. Crabtree, A/ARIBA

Recommended for special merit:
James Burford and Marshall A. Sisson, A/ARIBA
Percy Lingwood, ARIBA

Mendelsohn had arrived in England from Germany not eight months previously. In order to practise in Britain, he had teamed up with the young designer and architect Chermayeff, whose work on interiors at the BBC and whose position as a leading light of the Twentieth Century Group had already caught Mendelsohn's eye after Chermayeff had visited him several times in Berlin. On forming the partnership in the autumn of 1933, the pair

immediately started to collaborate on a number of projects brought to them by Chermayeff, whose connections within English society were both extensive and productive. The pavilion is, without doubt, their finest work.

Mendelsohn's designs for the Bexhill pavilion firmly established the practice at the forefront of British architecture. The vast majority of reviews were fulsome in their praise. "The assessor, Mr Thomas Tait, must have had little difficulty in choosing the winner", said *The Architects' Journal*. "Mr Mendelsohn and Mr Chermayeff have succeeded in making their solution tell on sight by their directness of approach to the problems involved and by the unaffected clarity of their drawings" (vol. 79, 8 February 1934, p. 205). The journal went on: "The stage has been miraculously set, and in all probability Bexhill will have not an immature tentative design, but one which will establish a criterion for the seaside architecture of the future." Tait himself felt that the designs "exhibited a masterly handling of architectural treatment".

Mendelsohn and Chermayeff's "masterly handling" becomes even clearer when the various entries are compared, a process open for all to do at the time since the entries were exhibited in two shows soon after the winners were announced, first at the York Hall, Bexhill, and subsequently at the Building Centre, London. For example, Haswell and Shepherd's design, which came second, had mixed towering structures first seen in such buildings as Dutchman Willem Dudok's Hilversum Town Hall (1924–30), with open, glass-fronted terraces redolent of the Swedish architect E. Gunnar Asplund's pavilions at the influential 1930 Stockholm Exhibition. However, placing the restaurant and sun terraces to the west of the proposed development meant that these fell directly in the shadow of the neighbouring Metropole Hotel, the bulky presence of which had been omitted from the original site plans reproduced in *The Architects' Journal*.

Freeman and Crabtree's design, in third place, chose an L-shaped solution, with the entertainments hall to the west and restaurant to the east. Its cantilevered façade clearly hinted at the kind of skill Crabtree was to demonstrate later in his design for

Below Though spectacular, Haswell and Shepherd's second-placed design was deemed too derivative of the other architects' work.

the Peter Jones department store (1936), itself a tribute to Mendelsohn's own ground-breaking work some ten years earlier for the Schocken stores in Germany. Interestingly, Mendelsohn himself seems to have first pondered a similar L-shaped solution, as early sketches of the pavilion plan now in the collection of his drawings held at the RIBA suggest.

Percy Lingwood's commended entry had a similar layout to the Haswell and Shepherd scheme, but paid less attention to the stipulation that the building should have a spacious entrance hall linking all the various elements together. Burford and Sisson, also commended, opted for an L-shaped layout like Freeman and Crabtree, yet the various elements of the design created some awkward axes, with sharp corners that would not only require some additional softening but could also present difficulties in windy weather, a frequent occurrence on England's south coast.

The quality of the entries is all the more obvious when one considers the calibre of the architects who did not even merit a commendation. For example, Earl De La Warr had himself invited the renowned architect Oliver Hill to enter the competition, so impressed had he been by Hill's Midland Hotel on the seafront in Morecambe, Lancashire, which had opened that year (1933). Maxwell Fry, too, was left off the list. Fry was, by now, vice-chairman of the MARS Group and a close associate of Chermayeff. Furthermore, his firm of Adams, Thomson & Fry had authored the original report that proposed the pavilion project. The firm's entry was grand, a curved restaurant partly surrounding a much-enlarged bandstand arena, but slightly complicated and, given that it required some fairly extensive moving of earth, almost certainly too expensive to construct. Perhaps driven by a desire to pursue his new commitment to Modernist principles, Fry left the practice later that year and subsequently established a brief partnership with Walter Gropius.

All the prize-winning or commended competition entries aligned their buildings to the shoreline, using a variety of configurations to provide access and open spaces, with differing levels of success. Mendelsohn and Chermayeff's scheme was simplicity itself. The design proposed three principal structural units: an entertainments hall, a restaurant and a main entrance hall linking the two that enabled them to be combined into a single architectural unit. Unlike many of the competing entries, Mendelsohn and Chermayeff's design seemed to anticipate the natural flow of visitors through the pavilion and, most importantly, allowed any part of the building to be used separately, if required.

Like his mentor, Frank Lloyd Wright, Mendelsohn had sought to integrate the building's design with its site, neatly using the site's sharp fall to the west for access to a basement under the stage of the auditorium. As the critic Arnold Whittick later commented: "Wright, it will be remembered, was very insistent on the unity of site and building and once remarked that no house should ever be built on a hill but should be of the hill. ... Mendelsohn always thoroughly studied the site and let its conditions partially determine the design" (Whittick 1956). This principle also extended to the building's horizontal shape and lines – a direct response to the horizon so clearly visible across the sea.

Elevation to Sea Front

Above Freeman and Crabtree's third-placed design captured the Modernist spirit, but the auditorium block and glazed restaurant wing created an awkward L-shape.

Mendelsohn's sketch of a spiral staircase, similar to the south staircase in the pavilion, survives in the Drawings Collection of the RIBA, suggesting that this, too, formed part of the early designs for the building. In true Modernist manner, two staircases were positioned to project, one at the front and one at the back of the pavilion's large, centrally placed entrance hall. These staircases gave access to every part of the building and perfectly balanced the pavilion's two main elements, the entertainments hall and the more relaxed catering and reading areas. Yet the sheer drama of the principal, south staircase served another purpose: placed at the end of the grand foyer, its swirling curves immediately invited visitors to ascend to the balcony, from where they gained an impressive view of the sea, to which the entire building is so clearly orientated. The north staircase worked in a different way, its circular form, with space alongside for poster displays and announcements of theatre performances, making an architectural focal point for visitors approaching from the town. Between the two staircases, the foyer provided a clear link between the town and the sea, an element missing from many of the other designs.

Mendelsohn originally proposed that the building be constructed in reinforced concrete, but his use of cantilevers, or steel beams, to support the exterior walls allowed his design to make maximum use of glass and, therefore, light. As in his earlier Schocken department stores, the pavilion's main supports were sited inside the building, with the cantilevers projecting from the supports and carrying great weights, much like a crane lifting weights on a building site. As a result, the winning design enabled the use of long lines of windows along the length of each floor, uninterrupted by support beams or columns, filling the building with sunlight along its restaurant, reading room or sun terraces.

Outside, the building's original designs worked equally well. The large entertainments hall successfully masked the back of the neighbouring Metropole Hotel from the view of the restaurant terrace, and, together with the projecting south staircase tower, offered protection from the prevailing westerly winds. To the east, Mendelsohn and Chermayeff proposed a glazed pergola, continuing on a level with the main restaurant terrace, thereby

ANOTHER VOTE IN FAVOUR.

RATEPAYERS' ASSOCIATION AND PAVILION SCHEME.

MAYOR'S CONVINCING SPEECH.

OPPOSITION OF ONE AT PUBLIC MEETING.

PALACE PROGRESS

Welded Steel Work at Bexhill

LARGEST IN ENGLAND

England's biggest welded steel erection, the Bexhill Marina Palace, is rapidly taking shape on the sea front.

After weeks of excavating in Bexhill's own particular brand of clay, the foundations are mostly in, the site has been levelled, and progress in the next few weeks should be rapid and impressive.

On Tuesday afternoon, with a minimum of fuss or excitement, the first of the four principal spans supporting the roof of the theatre was swung into position. Balanced on the giant sheer leg, it was manœuvred into place by a couple of men, and screwed home prior to being welded to the uprights.

WELDED GIRDERS

This welding business appears to be the big feature of the building, and it is arousing a good deal of interest among experts. As compared with the usual practice of bolting and riveting, its advocates claim that it has many advantages. In the first place, they estimate that at least 80 tons less steelwork is being employed at Bexhill than would have been the case with riveting. Secondly, it gives the architect more scope, and thirdly, by obviating the need to drill holes, it makes for greater strength in the girders.

Braithwaites, the famous steel people, of Newport (Mon.) and West Bromwich, are responsible for this part of the work. Actually as much as possible of the welding is done at the works, but natural difficulties of transport impose a limit. A welding plant is on the site, and the big sections are joined together before being lifted into place.

Putting in the foundations is at best a slow and difficult business, and in this case the contractor has been faced with a pretty problem.

It is not that of water. The site, apart from surface water, is splendidly dry. The trouble has lain with the soil, which (an "Observer" reporter was informed this week), is practically unique so far as the seaside is concerned. This is the blue clay, which you can see on the beach and on the South Cliff. When wet it breaks up into flakes, but when dry it has the consistency of rock and has to be attacked accordingly.

BEXHILL "ROCK"

Between ten and fifteen feet of this clay had to be excavated before the real rock was struck. Tests showed that when dry an inch square would support a pressure of ten tons, but when moistened it failed to hold a pressure of a ton.

Most of the excavating has had to be done at the Metropole end, and here the most progress has been made. The basement floor, with the boiler house, store rooms, etc., beneath the stage has been completed, although to the casual observer there does not seem to be much to show for it. That is explained by the fact that the walls are still being built up for the next floor, giving an unfinished appearance.

Each of the steel uprights for the hall, and for the glass sun parlours at the Devonshire-road end, stands on a concrete base from ten to fifteen feet in depth. When it is calculated how much clay had to be removed for each, and how many there are of them, it is hardly surprising that to mention Bexhill "rock" to a man on the job is, to put it mildly, anything but tactful.

ANTIQUE FURNITURE BOUGHT AND SOLD.—Sargents, 15, Sackville-road.

TO BUSINESS MEN!

A great tribute to Press advertising was paid by Mr. Richard Haigh, English manager of "His Master's Voice," at a private show in London of new radio instruments.

"There is absolutely no doubt in our minds that provided one has a good product at the right price Press Advertising is the cheapest way in which to sell it."

HAVE YOU SEEN Mastin's wonderful offer of pure silk on the front page?

SPECIAL OFFER

Another Little Error.

Another sample of the "arguments" that are being used against the Coastguard scheme is the statement that there are 500 empty houses in the town, the suggestion being, I suppose, that residents are leaving in large numbers, and that any addition to the rates would complete the evacuation.

If there were so many vacant properties in the town it would be an additional reason for the taking of measures to fill them. The number mentioned is, of course, a gross exaggeration. It was stated by the Mayor last Friday that the rateable value of empty houses was £15,000. This involves considerable loss to the rates, and it is a plausible contention that the cost of making Bexhill more attractive to residents might be offset by the money saved to the rates by a reduction of the number of empty houses.

The point to be remembered is that a standstill and do nothing policy may lead to a rise in the rates as well as constructive works for the improvement of the town.

Above and opposite From the day the building was first proposed, the pavilion has divided public opinion, as reports in the local newspapers bear witness.

BEXHILL BAY FROM THE PAVILION—A GROWING LOCAL INDUSTRY

Not the least of the many advantages of the De La Warr Pavilion is the commanding view afforded of Bexhill Bay with the background of the South Downs and Beachy Head. This photograph was taken with an extra red plate from the roof of the Pavilion.

"PRIVATE" OPPOSITION.

COASTGUARD SITE SCHEME.

BUSES ON THE FRONT.

At the meeting of the Commercial Society, which was held at the Devonshire Hotel on Monday evening, Mr. Harry Riley (the secretary) said he understood there had been a private meeting in the town to oppose the erection of a building on the Coastguard site.

The President (Councillor E. J. Bowles) remarked that he thought the town generally had been in favour of the proposal.

Mr. A. G. Luxton—That little private meeting will carry more weight than a public meeting. I will tell you what they will do. They will single out three or four of the more weak-kneed councillors, go for them, and they will change their minds.

The President questioned whether this was likely to happen, and Mr. Luxton added: "They will go for councillors individually and they will change their minds. You know the ones on the Council who like the limelight."

The President—I shall be very surprised if they change their minds in the face of what has gone forward

Mr. Luxton—I have known them change their minds between Council in Committee and the open Council.

The President—I think it will be a pity if there is strong opposition when the matter once gets started. It really wants the unanimous support of the whole town. I think the Council approached the matter in the right way when they threw it open for the public to discuss. They have had two or three opportunities.

BOWLS CUP.

PUBLIC SUPPORT FOR COUNCIL.

SEA FRONT DEVELOPMENT SCHEME.

WARNING AGAINST "SIDE-TRACKING."

The interest aroused by the Council's proposal to develop the Coastguard site by the erection, as the first stage of the scheme, of an entertainments hall at a cost not exceeding £50,000, was reflected by the large attendance at the public meeting held under the auspices of the Commercial Society at the Devonshire Hotel on Monday evening. There was an overwhelming body of opinion in favour of a forward move, although the view was advanced, principally by speakers associated with the Hotel and Boarding House Association, that another attempt should first be made to acquire the Pavilion site and clear away the amusement park. This proposal was evidently anticipated by Mr. H. L. Neale, who proposed a resolution endorsing the Council's action, and he made an appeal to the meeting not to be "side-tracked." The resolution was carried with eight dissentients.

Among those supporting the President (Councillor E. J. Bowles) were Councillor E. W. Bowrey, Councillor Colonel Stredinger, Colonel E. M. Liddell (chairman of the Ratepayers' Association), and the attendance also included Alderman R. C. Sewell, Councillor G. E. J. Foster, and Councillor F. Wimshurst.

"APT TO GET LOCALISED."

The President recalled that the Coastguard site had been purchased over a long period, and it now seemed that the time was ripe to take up the matter of its development and to see whether it was wise or otherwise to proceed. At the last meeting of the Council the Mayor ventilated the subject and he thought he put it in a very proper and a very strong manner. "He looks at things, naturally perhaps, free from such a local view as we do," added Councillor Bowles. "We are apt sometimes to get a little localised, and not to go far enough."

Traders hoped to reap some benefit from the scheme, because the more people that came to Bexhill the greater scope there was for trade; but it must be acknowledged also that it must be of some general benefit to the town. He thought one followed the other. Looking up the assessments, he found that traders and those interested in trade directly represented 26.83 per cent., dwelling houses 61.94, schools 4.53, the balance (6.70) being made up of Corporation and other properties. It might be said that 26 or 27 per cent. against 62 was only a small proportion, but it must be borne in mind that some properties came under the heading of factories and received de-rating relief, and he supposed that the majority of traders were also occupiers of dwelling houses. Employees probably occupied a good proportion of the dwellings, so he thought it would be fair to say that in a way traders represented half the assessments of the town, either directly or indirectly, through themselves or their dependants.

INTERESTS BOUND UP.

Apart from this consideration, Councillor Bowles contended that the interests of one section were bound up with the interests of the others; and he proceeded to quote the figures recently given by Alderman Bending (chairman of the Finance Committee of the Council) with regard to empty properties and the addition to the rateable value of new properties during the last two years. If they put the cost of the new building at £50,000 that would be a 2d. rate based on a 30 years' loan; and Councillor Bowles argued that if, as a result of a progressive policy they could get the "empties" filled up and the town continued to grow at the rate of the last two years, which had been very slow, there would be more than enough money, whichever way they took it, to provide this 2d. which was required for the loan.

A PROTEST.

At the conclusion of Councillor Bowles's speech, Mr. E. C. Short asked to be allowed to make a protest. He said that was a public meeting. About 32 minutes had elapsed; they had heard only one speech, and if they went on in that way members of the public who wished to say a word or two would not have the opportunity.

Councillor Bowles—You must not forget this is a Commercial Society meeting. They have the first claim, but they are not shutting out the public, I hope.

The resolution moved by Mr. Neale was in the following terms:—

"That this public meeting, called by the Bexhill Commercial Society, commits itself to support and co-operate in any scheme to place a building on the Coastguard site, to suitably house high-class music, conferences, concert parties, lectures and other social functions, and respectfully asks the Bexhill Corporation to take advantage of the present time, when, firstly, work is needed to ease the unemployment question; secondly, that building materials are cheaper; and, thirdly, that money is cheap.

"The society recommends that up to a twopenny rate be spent on this venture, to cover interest and repayment over a period of years. The building to contain a sun

will come, and now is the time to enable the Council to formulate their plans, and, when the time is ripe, to go ahead with them." (Applause.)

Mr. W. Spreag, seconding, said he had been a resident of the town for just on 30 years. He had seen a certain amount of progress, but he should very much like to see more.

A STEP FORWARD.

Mr. E. Fisher (manager of the Sackville Hotel) said he was afraid he was one of the "side-trackers," but he would like to say first of all that he thought the movement put forward was a step in the right direction. (Applause.) Anyhow, it was a step forward, but he considered a greater forward movement would be if the Council would decide to hold that plot for future development, and turn their attention to the old spot at the bottom of Sea-road. He knew that years ago it was the subject of discussion in the town, and that it was turned down by the people of Bexhill, but because a scheme had been once turned down it had not necessarily been turned down for good.

"I think that the key to the prosperity of Bexhill lies at the foot of Sea-road," said Mr. Fisher. "It is the centre of the parade; it is the most important part of it; it is everybody's terminus, and, from the business point of view, it is Bexhill. If this building is erected on the Coastguard site not everybody will see it. Every visitor to Bexhill does see the sea front and the beach; it is the object of their journeying. I speak on behalf of the Frederick Hotels, and also, I believe, on behalf of the Bexhill Hotel and Boarding House Association. I think they will tell you they have been taught by their visitors that from their point of view the situation on the sea front is a most vital problem facing Bexhill. (Applause.) Before £50,000 is spent on a new hall, I would suggest that the question of the sea front be re-examined, and if it is not possible to come to an agreement, then let us get on with the present proposal for a hall on the Coastguard site."

Miss Davis (manageress of the Granville Hotel) supported the view expressed by Mr. Fisher, and said that visitors were continually passing remarks about that "dreadful place at the bottom of Sea-road," and asking what the Council were doing to allow such a place. She thought it was a disgrace to any first-class seaside town, and she did not believe that Bexhill would ever progress very far until something was done about that site.

CONFUSING THE ISSUE.

Mr. A. H. Stone thought this was confusing the issue, and that the two points could be dealt with separately. "I believe the Bexhill Corporation should proceed with that entertainments hall," he added. "They have pandered these last five to ten years to certain people, mostly, I suppose, retired mayors and captains of the Indian Army. There are a number of people with limited incomes in Bexhill, but they are only a minority, and surely they are not to be allowed to dictate the policy of Bexhill. I should like to see this scheme go forward. It is stated in the resolution that it would ease unemployment, and God knows that wants easing. Materials are cheaper to-day than they have ever been, and money is cheap. Surely it is the ideal time. No town can stand still; it either goes forward or back. Since I have been in Bexhill it has gone back—probably due to my influence (laughter)—I want to see it go forward. Those people who wish to live on parochial incomes and yet have the benefit of a modern seaside town, should try Peacehaven or somewhere like that, and not try to scotch a progressive borough."

Mr. Stone also expressed the hope that when the time came the Council would make adequate provision for those people living at the present on the Coastguard site.

Mr. Peckham said he was in part agreement with the remarks of Mr. Fisher, but he did feel most strongly that they should not let the site at the bottom of Sea-road confuse the issue regarding this hall. (Applause.) He thought the question whether they required this hall or not was answered most decidedly by any who cared to go to Hastings, when there was a special musical festival or anything like that, and saw the number of cars which left the Hastings pavilion and came home Bexhill way. (Hear, hear.)

Mr. H. W. Howard said he was wondering whether the go-ahead Corporation could see their way to take in hand both schemes.

"WAKE UP, BEXHILL."

Mr. Funnell thought the position was summed up on the placard of the "Bexhill Observer"—"Wake up, Bexhill."

Mr. William Meads, of St. Leonards, who said he had been connected with Bexhill longer than anyone in the room, praised the Coastguard site, but advocated the building of a Town Hall there which could be used for all the officials. At Hastings they had masking from view a rather odd collection of buildings. The pergola was linked to the existing colonnade and bandstand, incorporating them into the design and thus providing a further connection between the building and the shoreline.

The building was unquestionably 'modern' in appearance, its design modular, functional and efficient. Its flat roof contrasted starkly with the raked roofs of the neighbouring Edwardian terraces; its windows, which the architects suggested be framed in rust-resistant bronze, were arranged in horizontal strips in line with the building's shape; and any functional elements, such as staircases or displays, were placed prominently on the exterior, which, it was proposed, would be rendered in white.

Architect and Building News claimed that in 1925 "the three great names in modern architecture were Gropius, Le Corbusier and Mendelsohn" (vol. 144, 20 December 1935, p. 343). With the pavilion project, Bexhill would be the first town in Britain to secure an example of one of these masters' works. This significance was not lost on *The Architects' Journal*, which commented: "It appears to us that Mr Tait's award at Bexhill may have far-reaching effects on the progress of contemporary design in this country. The Bexhill Corporation is to be congratulated on having initiated the first modern competition of any size to be held in this country" (vol. 79, 8 February 1934). But, presciently, the article added: "We hope that they will allow none of the obvious devices of obstructionists or disgruntled persons to interfere with the realization of the first premiated design, which is, in the opinion of those who have seen it, a work of outstanding merit."

The writer of the article could not have known it, but the feared 'interference' was just about to begin. The first objections to the winning design focused not on the calibre of the entry, but on the nationality of its creators. As in Germany, in Britain in the early 1930s supporters of socialism and those of fascism were engaged in an ideological tussle. Even Bexhill's socialist mayor could count the leader of the newly formed British Union of Fascists, Oswald Mosley, as a friend and former Labour Party colleague. Architecture was not immune to the ideology of the far right. Barely

had a week passed after the winning designs were announced than a small yet highly vocal group of fascist architects began to sound off in articles about this latest 'injustice' to their profession; their views were first published in the *Fascist Week* and subsequently reprinted in *The Architects' Journal*: "The Royal Institute of British Architects, whose primary duty is presumably to protect the interests of British Architects, betrays them by encouraging professional activities in this country of those aliens who have found it advisable to flee from their own land. ... The planning of our future towns lies before us as an immense and glorious opportunity. Britons, not aliens, shall carry out the task" (vol. 79, 15 February 1934, p. 244). The council came in for further criticism, with the town clerk being attacked by local resident Walker Heath in protest against "the employment of an alien architect for the erection of a building by a public body to the exclusion of British architects" (*ibid.*).

Earl De La Warr, who had prepared such a careful campaign to enable the project to proceed, had perhaps foreseen such criticism and was ready to respond to it. That week he rattled off a swift reply that was printed in both *The Architects' Journal* and the *Bexhill-on-Sea Observer*: "You are no doubt aware that in a competition of this character no one, not even the Council or the Assessor himself, knows the names of the competitors until the award has actually been made" (*The Architects' Journal*, vol. 79, 15 February 1934, p. 244; *Bexhill-on-Sea Observer*, 10 February 1934, p. 4). Describing Mendelsohn as "one of the greatest architects on the continent before he was turned out of Germany by the present regime", the earl went on to stress that, if the architect were to stay in Britain and apply for naturalization, he was given to understand that the RIBA "would be pleased to consider him for the bestowal of the highest honour that the profession could give".

However hard De La Warr might campaign, there were many residents in Bexhill for whom the thought of a foreign architect designing their new pavilion was unpalatable. And their principal line of attack was the building's escalating cost. By the end of the month, De La Warr had already seen off the first criticisms, defusing concerns that the inhabitants of the coastguard cottages that were still standing on the site would need to be rehoused by reminding critics that new council accommodation had been promised when the project was first mooted.

A second financial matter was less easily resolved. When the scheme was first approved the council had authorized a budget of £50,000, representing a 2*d*. increase in local rates. A month into the competition, this figure had been increased to £60,000 to accommodate the cost of necessary stage equipment. Allowing for increased estimates for the subsequent running of the building, and the loss of rateable income deriving from the coastguard cottages, the rate increase rose to 5*d*.

To assuage concerns from the ratepayers' association, the council decided to apply to the Ministry of Health for a loan to cover the £80,000 cost now estimated for the building. (At the time, the government encouraged activities and facilities that it believed promoted the good health of the nation, and the Ministry of Health therefore offered financial support to projects dedicated to the pursuit of outdoor recreation.) Aware of the local concerns, the ministry insisted on holding a public inquiry into the scheme before authorizing any such loan. The future of the building was to be decided in a two-day inquiry held at Bexhill Town Hall on 5 and 6 April 1934. At their new offices in Oxford Street in London, Mendelsohn and Chermayeff began work on modifying the designs in accordance with Tait's report. Tait had made two recommendations, both of which were taken up by Mendelsohn. The first involved creating a separate corridor connecting the north and south staircases on the first floor, to provide better access to the lecture hall and reading room on one side and the entertainments hall gallery on the other. The second was that the bandstand area might be reconsidered with a view to the future development of the scheme. Mendelsohn's reaction was to propose that, rather than merely linking the bandstand with the pavilion via the two-storey pergola, the bandstand itself should be remodelled to form a circular swimming pool, thus responding to the then fashionable notion of the health-giving properties of sea air, swimming and sunshine. From this pool would extend a two-level pier, continuing the pergola theme, with a tall, steel pylon at the end, which, in some of Mendelsohn's drawings, also appears like a statue of a diver.

The biggest change introduced during this period involved the building's actual construction technique. In their original winning designs, Mendelsohn and Chermayeff proposed using conventional reinforced concrete construction. Yet Mendelsohn would have been aware of cheaper ways to achieve the same strength. In September 1933 the renowned Austrian-born engineer Felix Samuely had arrived in Britain, ostensibly to visit an exhibition. Samuely was already celebrated for designing, among other achievements, the first all-welded steel-framed building in Berlin and had previously worked with Mendelsohn on a similarly engineered project for the Josty Haus, a circular building proposed, but never realized, for Berlin's Potsdamer Platz. On hearing of Samuely's arrival, Mendelsohn was quick to contact his former associate to see if he could come up with ideas for the new project in Bexhill.

Below The architects' model for the building is on long-term loan to the Victoria and Albert Museum, London. When it was displayed in Bexhill in 1934 it was the first time the public had seen the architects' plans to augment the pavilion with a two-storey pergola linking to a circular swimming pool and a pier out to sea.

When the inquiry opened in April, therefore, the architects had improved their original proposals. Occupying a prominent spot in the middle of the town-hall chamber was a new model of the proposed scheme, something rare in British architecture at the time, although used by Mendelsohn for many years in Germany. People could actually see what the architect's expressive sketches and design drawings would look like in three dimensions, together with the proposed amendments involving the pergola, pier and swimming pool. Mendelsohn and Chermayeff also enlisted the help of a young quantity surveyor, Cyril Sweett, who calculated the material and construction costs of the building with an eye for detail that would have been impossible for Mendelsohn to capture: having arrived in Britain only ten months earlier, Mendelsohn had yet to grasp the difference between feet and metres, let alone work out the cost of concrete and steel in pounds, shillings and pence.

It was not until the inquiry opened that the public learned for the first time that the architects were proposing an entirely new way, for Britain at least, of constructing the building's inner frame: Samuely had suggested using steel rather than concrete, and welding it together rather than using rivets. Light, quick to construct and therefore significantly less expensive, the building would be the first of its kind in the country. Aside from keeping the costs of construction to a minimum, the use of welded steel also had an aesthetic impact. Its increased strength enabled greater loads to be placed on the joints, with the resulting reductions in joint and beam size allowing the use of thinner and more streamlined walls and floors.

Mendelsohn himself took no part in the inquiry, largely owing to the fact that he was still struggling with the English language. He attended each day, however, and, according to Sweett, "thoroughly enjoyed" it. While Earl De La Warr and several other witnesses were called to give evidence, it was left to Chermayeff to field most of the questions. "Under cross examination he [Chermayeff] was not very convincing and gave wrong answers to some questions which I corrected until cross-examining Counsel protested and requested that the Inspector asked to keep me quiet", explained Sweett in later years. "The Inspector, however, replied that I seemed to know more about the detail of the building than Mr Chermayeff and it would probably be helpful if I joined him in the witness box, which I then did" (*Erich Mendelsohn 1887–1953* 1987, p. 69).

The aids of the model, new construction techniques and other savings notwithstanding, the inspector's hands were tied to a degree: the Local Government Act of 1929 allowed a maximum annual rate increase of only 4*d*. It was clear that certain items had to go. On 28 September the inspector announced his decision, sanctioning a loan of £70,000 for the project to be repaid over thirty years, with a further £8412, to be repaid over fifteen years. These budgetary constraints were used in future years by opponents of the scheme both to curtail proposals to extend the scheme further and to keep a close check on the costs of the pavilion's maintenance and entertainments programme.

Nevertheless, Bexhill – and Earl De La Warr in particular – had succeeded in getting the pavilion project under way. Technologically advanced and designed by a master architect, the pavilion finally offered Bexhill an opportunity to compete seriously with neighbouring towns for tourists. Like attractions in many of those towns, the enterprise had been funded by the municipal authority, although not without criticism. Moreover, the project had a clear social purpose: to bring prosperity to the townsfolk and to enlighten the public with the quality of the pavilion's design and its entertainments programme. The pavilion was not just going to be a fine addition to the Sussex coastline; it was going to be world-class.

pavilion drawings and sketches

The sketches and plans in this section follow the development of the De La Warr Pavilion from the architects' early concepts to the final designs.

Top left An early sketch demonstrates how Mendelsohn struggled with the original layout of the building.

Top right Perspective sketches such as this one, with their ground-level viewpoints, accentuate the site's contours and add drama to the building's appearance.

Bottom Another early sketch shows the importance Mendelsohn placed on vertical axes – here, a flagpole and the proposed statue for the south terrace.

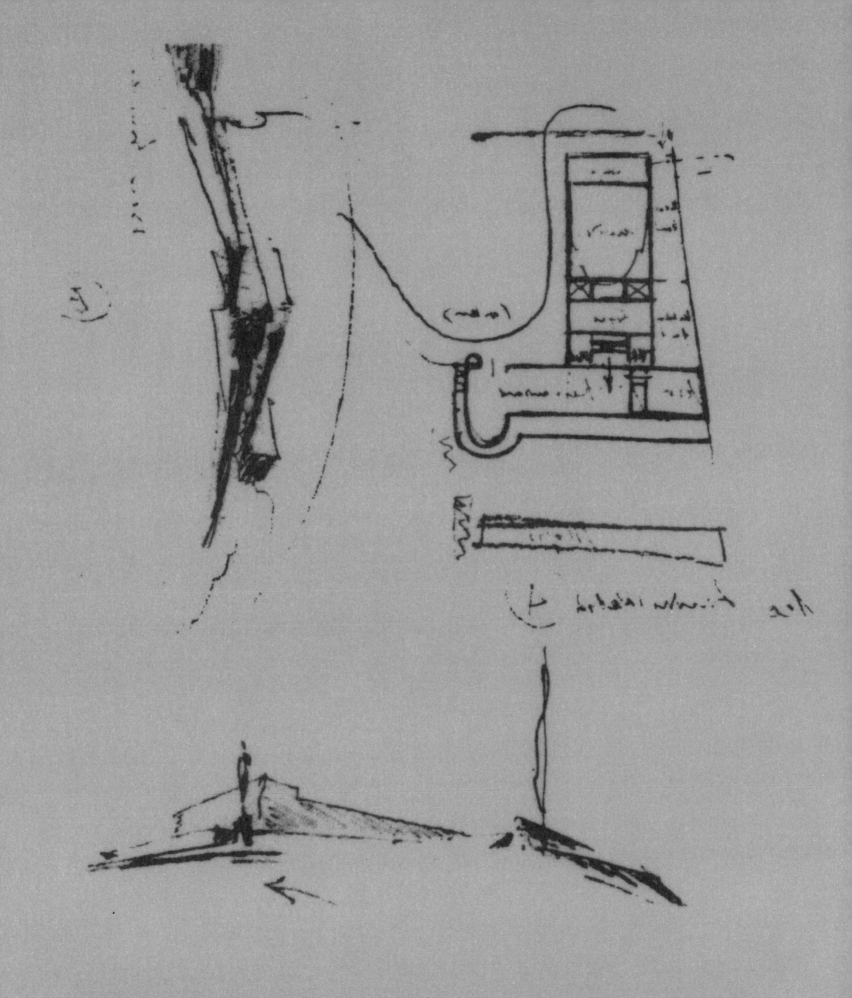

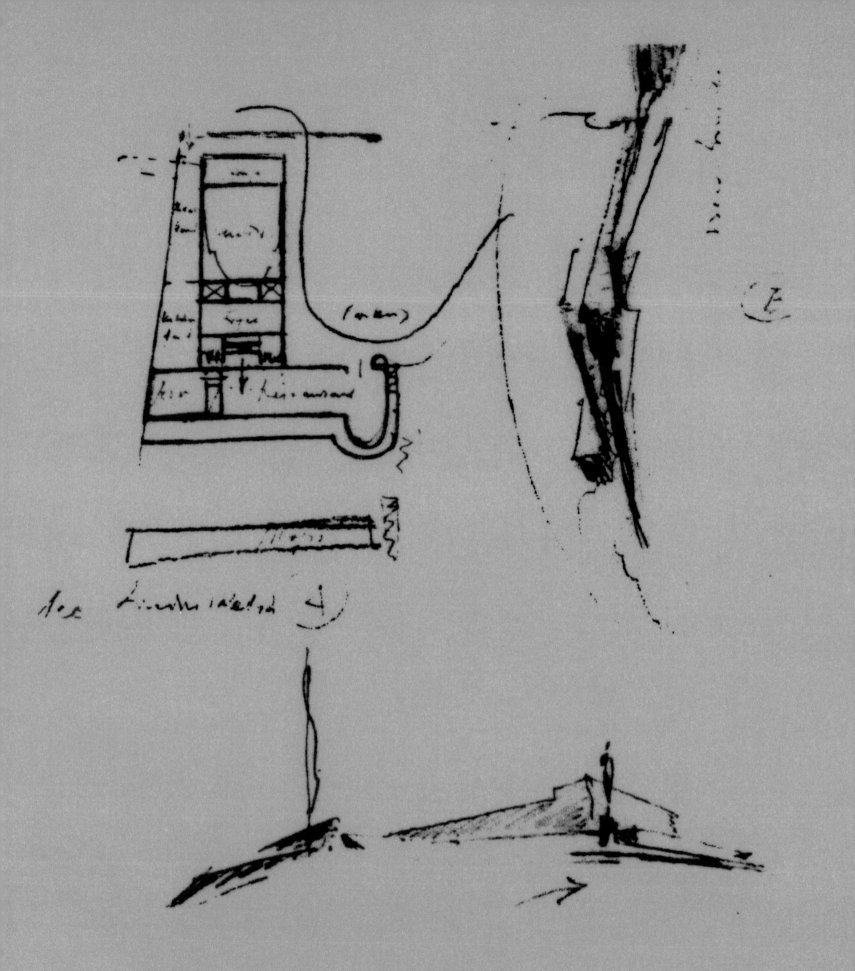

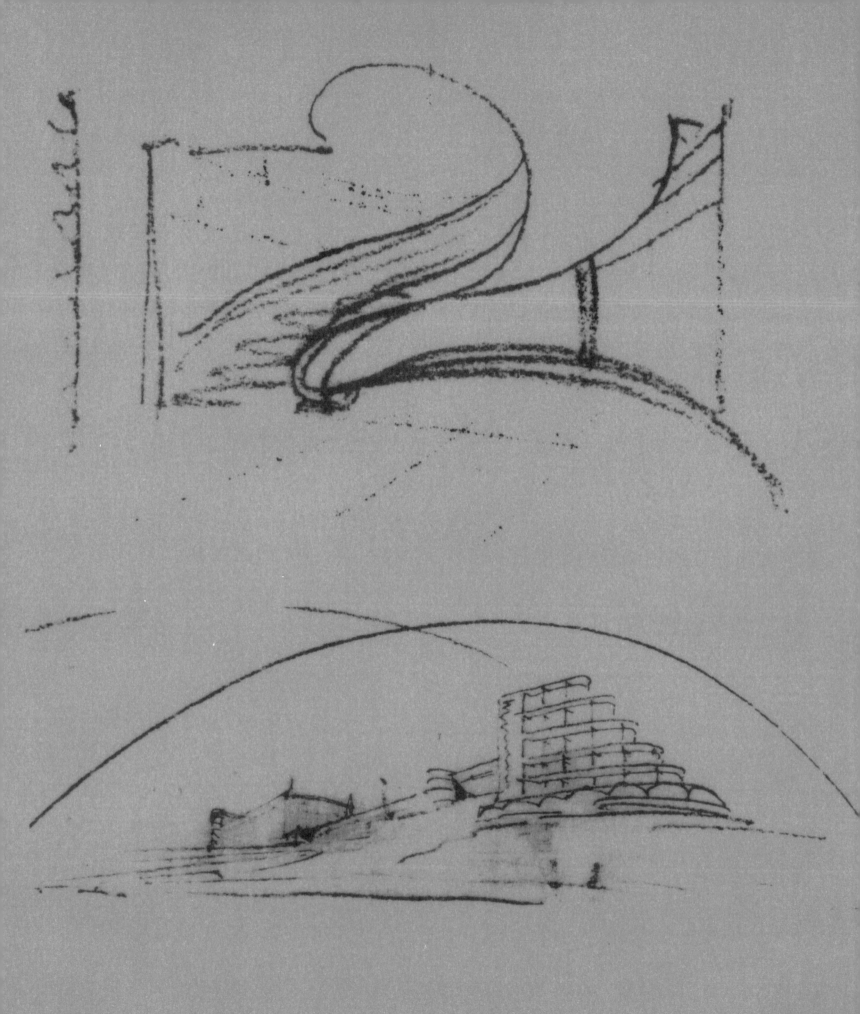

Top Curved staircases became
a familiar feature of Mendelsohn's work.
The staircase eventually built at Bexhill
spiralled in the opposite direction.

Bottom A later drawing, from about
1934, shows the proposed hotel
development for the south-western
end of the pavilion.

Top Later drawings, dating from about 1934, show a line of windows across the top of the auditorium.

Bottom The north aspect: the final design takes shape.

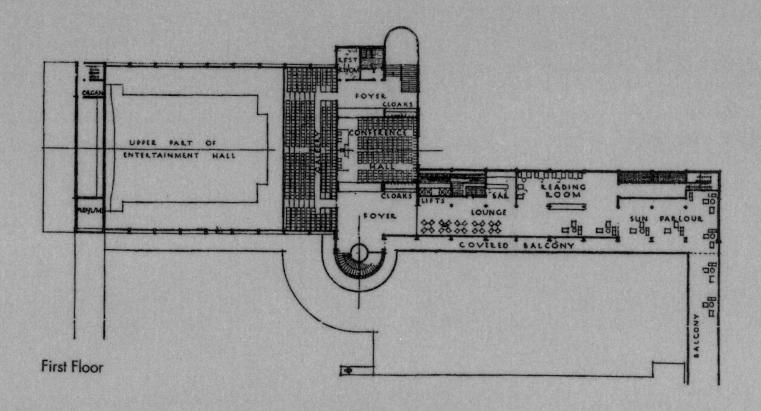

First Floor

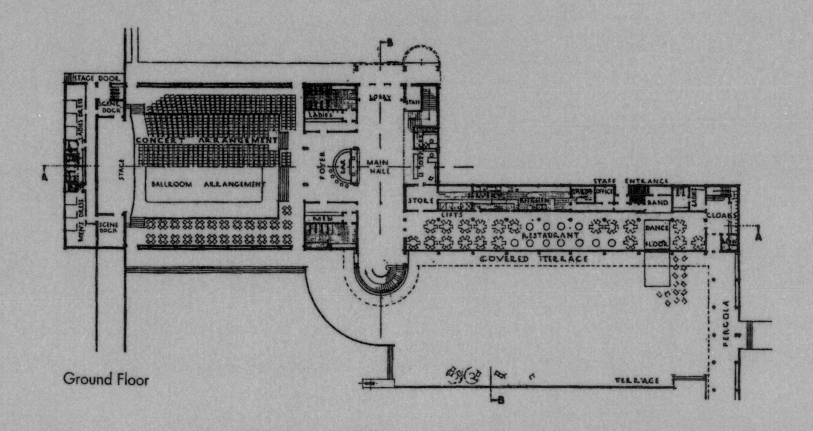

Ground Floor

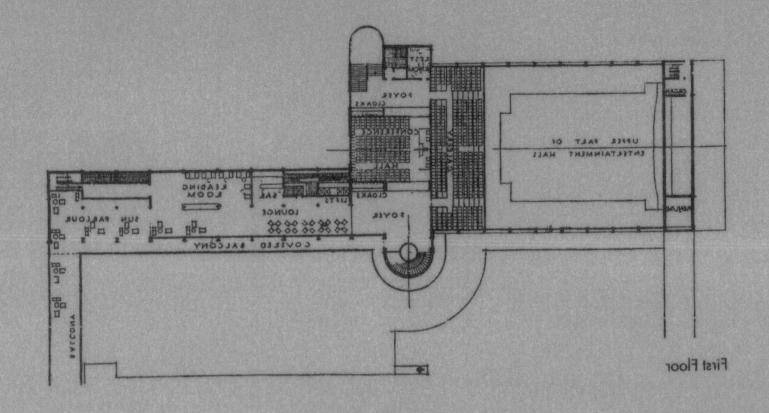

First Floor

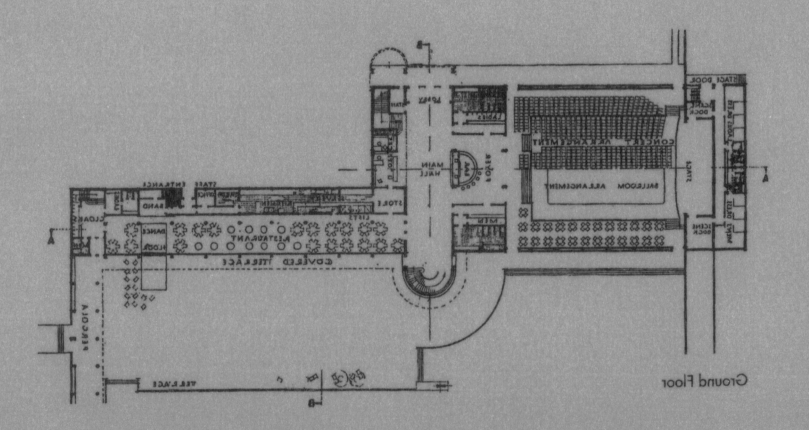

Ground Floor

Top The original plan shows the conference hall dividing the north and south terraces. At the assessor Thomas Tait's suggestion, the hall was reduced in size and a corridor introduced to connect the two.

Bottom The winning design was commended for enabling all areas of the building to be accessed from the large entrance hall, which had staircases at either end. The flexible seating arrangements for the auditorium also won praise.

Top This plan shows the pavilion as it was built. Provision had been made for a deeper stage and more backstage areas, but a bar, originally proposed for the auditorium foyer, had disappeared.

Bottom The architects had added more seats in the gallery, but the rake of the seating meant that the ceiling height of the auditorium wing had to be raised.

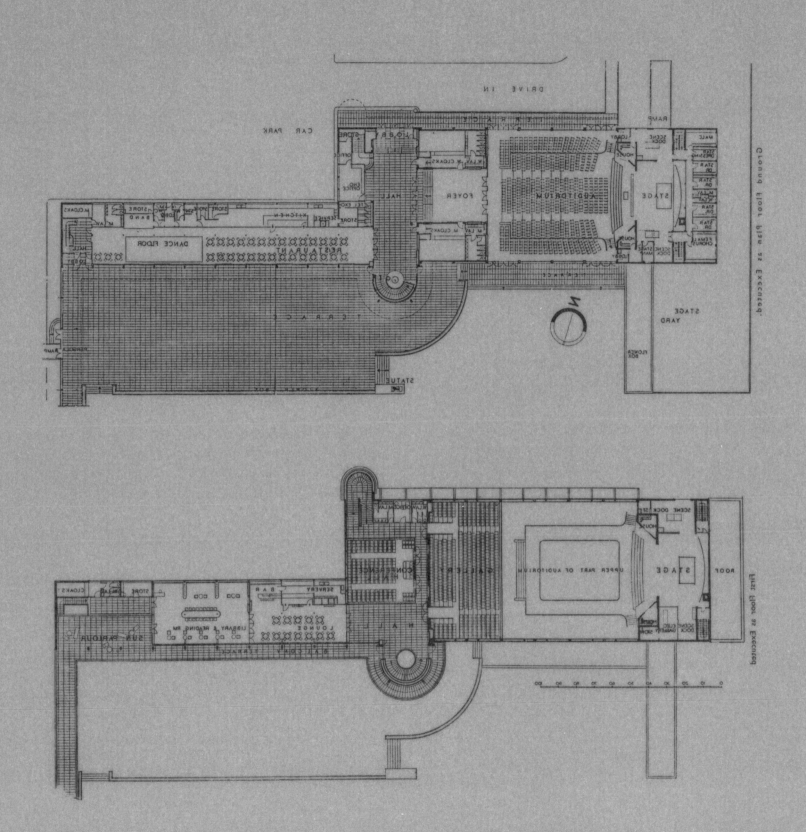

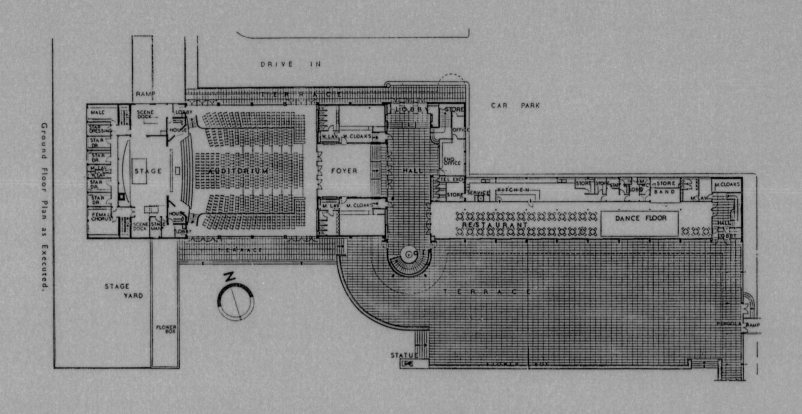

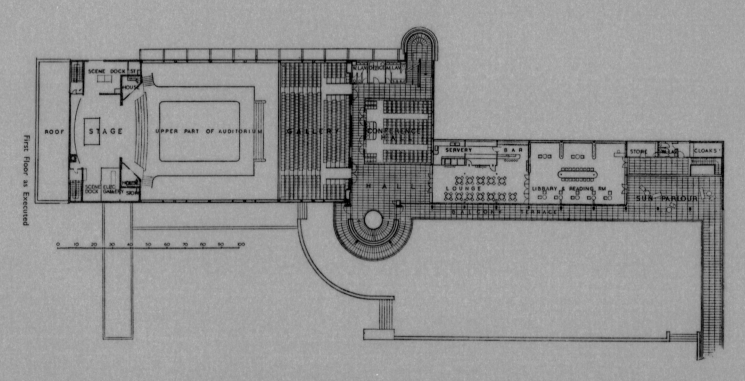

Ground Floor Plan as Executed.

DRIVE IN

CAR PARK

RAMP

MALE

STAGE

SCENE DOCK

LOBBY

HOUSE

TERRACE

AUDITORIUM

FOYER

HALL

LOBBY

STORE

OFFICE

W. LAV.

W. CLOAKS

ENQ. OFFICE

TEL. EXCH.

STORE

SERVICE

KITCHEN

STORE

STORE

STAFF

M. WC.

LOBBY

STORE

BAND

M. CLOAKS

M. LAV.

HALL LOBBY

RESTAURANT

DANCE FLOOR

STAR DRESSING

STAR DR.

STAR DR.

M. LAV. W. LAV.

STAR DR.

STAR DR.

FEMALE CHORUS

SCENE DOCK

STAGE MAN

HOUSE

LOBBY

M. LAV.

M. CLOAKS

TERRACE

STAGE YARD

N

TERRACE

PERGOLA RAMP

FLOWER BOX

STATUE

FLOWER BOX

First Floor as Executed

ROOF

SCENE DOCK

ST

HOUSE

STAGE

UPPER PART OF AUDITORIUM

GALLERY

W. LAV. OFFICE M. LAV.

CONFERENCE HALL

SERVERY

BAR

STORE

CLOAKS

SCENE DOCK

ELEC GALLERY

HOUSE

STORE

HALL

LOUNGE

LIBRARY & READING RM

SUN PARLOUR

BALCONY TERRACE

0 10 20 30 40 50 60 70 80 90 100

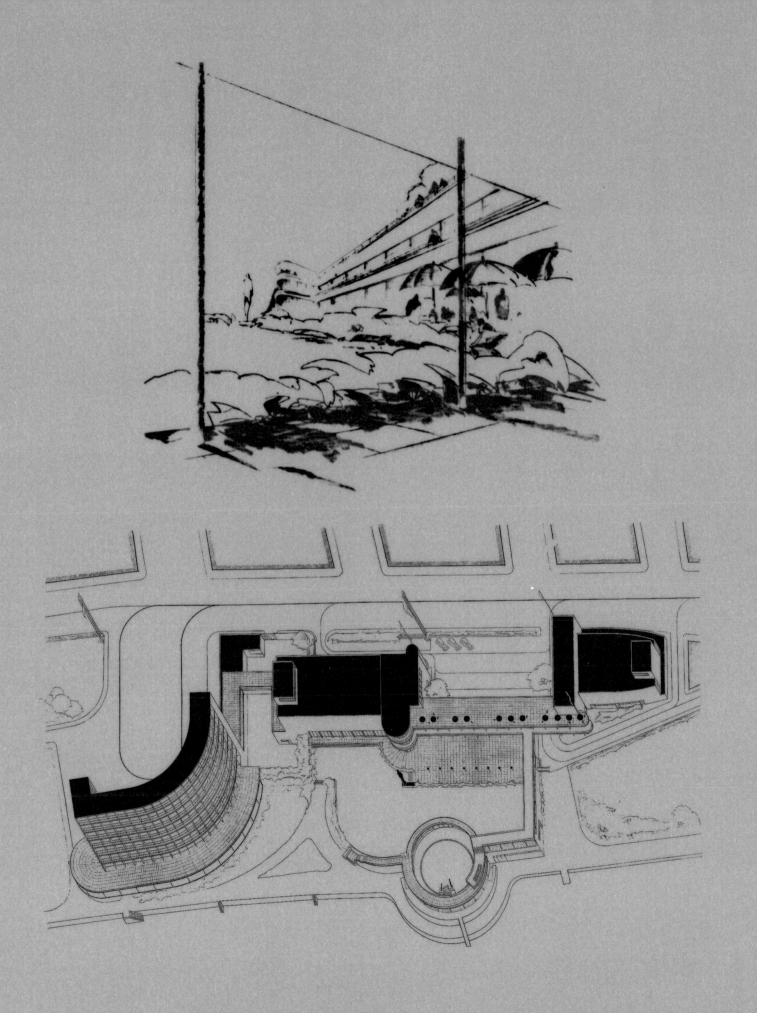

Top The proposed two-storey pergola frames the south terrace.

Bottom Later plans, published in *Architectural Review* in 1936, included proposals for a hotel to the west and a cinema to the east – in effect, a complete cultural resort for visiting guests.

The construction of the De La Warr Pavilion started in January 1935, and by February the steel frames of both the restaurant and the auditorium blocks were already well advanced. The building took only eleven months to complete, demonstrating the efficiency of the new techniques that Mendelsohn and Samuely had brought to Britain.

Although the use of welded steel was being considered at the time – indeed, the London County Council had just approved it for its own buildings – no one in the country had actually employed it before. But Mendelsohn and Samuely knew precisely what they were doing; to them, the construction technique was tried and tested and, as pioneers of the International Style, as it came to be known, they knew it could be adopted outside Germany.

That the pavilion emerged more or less as visualized by its architects, however, had as much to do with those responsible for its execution as with its designers, since its design, which stressed the continuity of the interior spaces through unbroken, flush ceilings, balconies and projecting floors of minimum (and uniform) thickness, posed practical problems from an engineering perspective.

In addition to Samuely, Mendelsohn had added a third foreigner to the team, the Austrian Johannes (Hannes) Schreiner, who had been Mendelsohn's chief assistant in Berlin and had followed him over from the Continent and joined the practice late in 1934. Schreiner and Samuely were old friends from Germany and knew each other's work well, Schreiner frequently referring to his engineering colleague as "the penguin" due to his shape and gait. The young English architect Birkin Haward had also joined the practice as a junior draughtsman, offering his services to Mendelsohn fresh from architecture school in 1934 and subsequently being taken on to work with Schreiner to develop the pavilion's entertainments hall elevations and working drawings. It was to this team, therefore, that much of the detailed design work fell, to bring the partners' designs into reality.

Much debate has focused on how the two partners divided up responsibility for the project. When first admitted to the RIBA,

Chermayeff proclaimed his profession on headed notepaper as "interior architect", although this term may prove less informative when it comes to the pavilion. Certainly, his experience as an architect had hitherto been restricted to but one construction, a modest, three-bedroom house for Mr and Mrs Shann in Rugby, Warwickshire (1933–34), built for £1000. Many of the features of the pavilion's design were pure Mendelsohn: its balanced approach, its central, circular staircase and the incorporation of its name as a key feature of the building's façade.

In his 'Recollections of the Mendelsohn & Chermayeff Practice' (1988), Haward recalls that Mendelsohn would spend many hours at the drawing-board, working on design sketches that his associates, Haward included, would then be charged with developing into scale plans. Haward was also in charge of Mendelsohn's gramophone, on which were played his beloved Bach concertos and sonatas while he worked: "Sometimes he would require one particular movement to be repeated over and over most of the morning. It was an education for me and I enjoyed it, but SC [Serge Chermayeff] got rather tired of this at times (to put it mildly)."

Mendelsohn clearly had a very different way of working to Chermayeff. Joan Ridge, their secretary at the time, when interviewed many years later by the Pavilion Trust, recounted that "Mr Chermayeff was a Socialite. He knew all the grand and theatrical people and was always out a lot during the day. It seemed it was Mr Mendelsohn who did all the solid work on the pavilion. Nevertheless, Mr Chermayeff was mainly responsible for the interior decoration, as great an attraction as the building itself" (*Pavilion Trust Newsletter*, July 1998, p. 2).

Although it had been the simplicity of the building's design and layout that had so impressed Thomas Tait, the engineering of such simplicity was a difficult task. The pavilion's design employed many innovative techniques completely untried in Britain. Mendelsohn included cantilevered walls in his design, which he had previously used to great effect in his Schocken department store in Chemnitz, in order to achieve the light, clean lines to which he aspired.

Below, top As at Bexhill, the cantilevers of Mendelsohn's
Schocken department store in Chemnitz, supporting the
building load, allowed glass walls to be used to full effect.

Below, centre The demolition of the old
coastguard cottages begins in Bexhill
in January 1935.

Bottom Off-site prefabrication of the
frames meant that construction of the
pavilion was swift.

And with the joints now being welded, rather than riveted, floor lines and supports could become even more slender. The pavilion's balconies, it seemed, would float in the air.

Notes on the building's frame, written by Samuely while the pavilion was under construction in 1935, started to appear in the journal *The Welder*. Unsurprisingly, the welding profession expressed strong interest in the new solutions that the pavilion offered. It is clear that the construction of the building was driven by its design. For example, the position of the proposed conference room on the pavilion's first floor posed a problem. The room was designed to rise through the first and second floors of the building, yet had to be kept clear of supports at the second-floor level so that light could enter from its clerestory windows. At the same time, enclosing it with partition walls to the north, west and south sides (where there was to be a screen of folding doors) made it impossible to extend the ground-floor columns up to the roof. Samuely's solution was to suspend the second-floor steelwork from girders placed in the roof.

This solution provided the key to many of the other conundrums posed by Mendelsohn's quest for a sleek, uniform and refined look. The building's south façade, for example, is a paragon of construction innovation. In his original design, Mendelsohn drew the two balconies that encircle the south staircase as being supported on only two slender columns, with the balcony lines carried all along the building's eastern wing, giving it its liner-like appeal. Building slender balconies in a straight line is relatively straightforward. Carrying those same lines around a circular, curved-glass feature, on the other hand, involved preventing the balcony twisting out of shape. The problem was overcome by constructing a section with a very heavy web – the girders around the circular balconies are 25 cm (10 in.) thick to prevent twisting – while the two columns were built up into very strong box-sections within the limits allowed by the design. The heavy beams of the circular balconies were then supported by cantilevers at each floor level, consisting of two channels with additional plates, which were then welded to each side of the box-column as it rose through the building. The effect of the slender circular balconies from within is striking: despite being

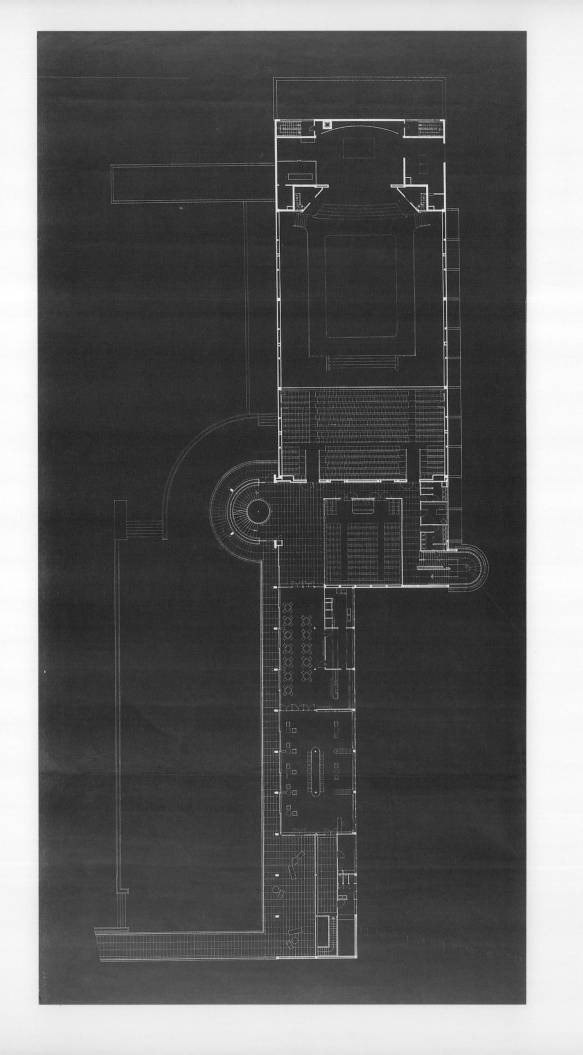

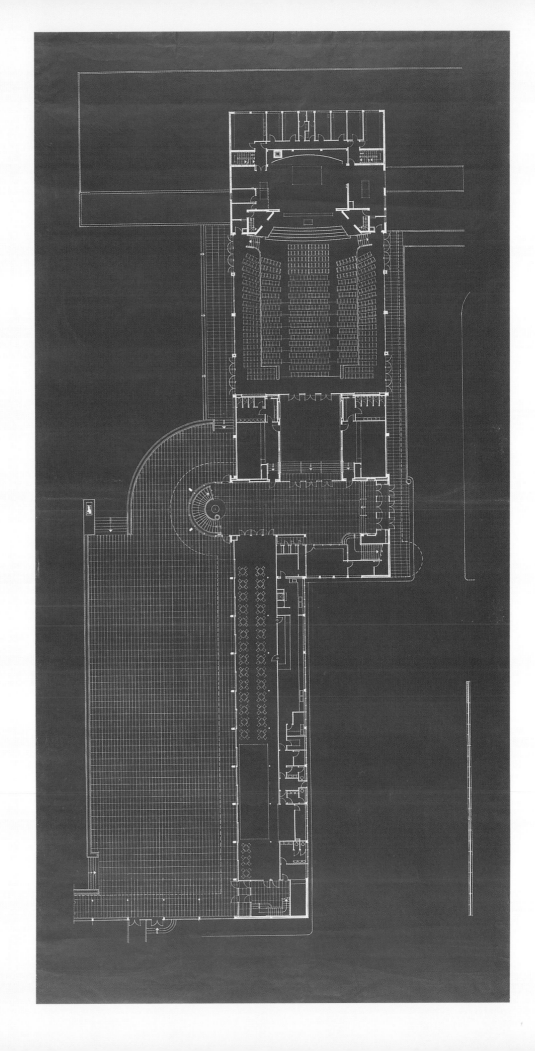

Opposite and right Both Mendelsohn's and Chermayeff's plans were destroyed during the Second World War. Only these blueprints remain in the RIBA Drawings Collection.

Below By exploiting the main slope of the site, the design kept earthworks to a minimum.

Bottom, left The first of the main structural columns is lifted into place in January 1935.

Bottom, right A 15-cm (6-in.) bed of concrete covers the entire floor base in March 1935.

both heavy and strong, they seem to float in mid-air around a cylinder of glass. Since it was comparatively light, the steelwork carrying the curved-glass panels of the semicircular wall enclosing the staircase was built to be suspended from the roof steel above. The north staircase, too, owes its look and appeal to the cantilevered construction, with the floors, stairs, glass and walls all suspended by hangers cantilevered from the main roof girders.

Once Mendelsohn and the engineering team had arrived at these design solutions, the building work began. The coastguard cottages occupying the site were demolished using steamrollers that dragged anchored steel cabling through the buildings. The foundations of the columns were the first to be laid – reinforced concrete shafts with splayed spreaders at their feet – and they were then connected by reinforced concrete ground-beams where they needed to support walls or parts of the basement slabs. Some of the walls, too, were made of reinforced concrete, particularly around the auditorium, since the heavy roof and sloping ground required them to carry significant loads. Around the columns, a 15-cm (6-in.) bed of concrete was laid over the entire area of the building, while under both the ground-beams and the whole stage area, an underbed, or blinding, 8 cm (3 in.) thick, was laid to receive a layer of asphalt. Surprisingly, for a site situated so close to the shore and built largely on clay, there is no record of any difficulties having been encountered with the foundations.

Above ground level, a more novel approach to building techniques was adopted. Many of the solutions chosen in the construction were experimental. With the benefit of hindsight, critics can now see the flaws in some of the decisions taken. Without experience of the techniques and the behaviour of the new materials, much of the construction of the pavilion represented little more than a leap in the dark, a daring escapade on which town, architect and builder alike were venturing.

The firm of Rice & Sons from Brighton had been appointed as general building contractor. It was given fifty weeks to complete the task, with the proviso that as much local labour as possible be employed on the construction of the pavilion. For much of the early construction, therefore, Rice & Sons turned to the nearby fishing town of Hastings for labour. The welded-steel frame technique meant that large sections of the building could be prefabricated elsewhere and brought to the site ready for erection. As a result, the Braithwaite Welding & Construction Company welded many of the girders and frames for the pavilion at its depot, transporting them to the site only when they were needed – a working method that was a complete innovation at the time. However, prefabricated frames brought the problem of how to raise the heavy sections to their desired positions. It was the fishermen labourers of Rice & Sons, with their centuries-long tradition of hauling their flat-bottomed fishing boats on to the beach with block and tackle, who came up with the solution. Slowly and laboriously, the massive beams were each lifted into place and bolted or welded together. By the spring of 1935, the entire frame had been constructed. Flanked on three sides by a mixture of Victorian and Edwardian buildings, the pavilion's steel skeleton rising from the foundations was a shocking sight for many of the local residents. Nothing of its kind had ever been seen before. As the *Bexhill-on-Sea Observer* noted: "In the early stages of construction, the unaccustomed horizontal lines and austerity of the outside walls were somewhat disturbing to conventional ideas of entertainment halls" (14 December 1935, p. 11).

Other aspects of the construction were also unconventional. Instead of being located on the building site itself, the headquarters for the operation were the elegant surroundings of the Cooden Beach Hotel, owned and run by the 9th Earl's wife, Diana. There the team of builders, architects and engineers developing the pavilion gathered for meetings to discuss progress on the construction a couple of miles along the coast. It was also from Cooden Beach that King George V and Queen Mary set out to visit the building site. During a lunch party at the hotel, the royal couple were so taken with the model of the pavilion that a visit to the site was hurriedly arranged by the earl.

By 6 May 1935, the day of the king's silver jubilee, the building was ready for the laying of its foundation plaque. Gathered together beneath the steel skeleton of the construction, the mayor, his wife and children and other assembled dignitaries placed underneath the plaque a sealed tube time-capsule containing a copy of the *Bexhill-on-Sea Observer* and a list of the names of the foremen and general staff of the builders who were employed on the site. The socialist mayor was not only celebrating the achievements of the workers, however. In his speech, he revealed the true spirit in which the venture was being undertaken: "I mark a great day in the history of Bexhill, for which we have rightly chosen a great day in the history of our nation. How better could we dedicate ourselves today than by gathering round this new venture of ours, a venture which is going to lead to the growth, the prosperity and the greater culture of this, our town." He added, significantly: "... a venture also which is part of a great national movement virtually to found a new industry – the industry of giving that relaxation, that pleasure, that culture, which hitherto the gloom and dreariness of British resorts has driven our fellow countrymen to seek in foreign lands". Like so many buildings that were to follow it, Earl De La Warr's new pavilion had a visionary as well as a utilitarian purpose.

The principal architects were not frequently seen on site, Mendelsohn himself only twice during the construction period. He was busy developing a new architectural practice in Palestine after being approached by his old friend Professor Chaim Weizmann, the head of the Zionist Organization, to build him a house in Rehovot. As more commissions came in, Mendelsohn frequently undertook the three-day flight to the Middle East from his London base, leaving Chermayeff to oversee the office and keep him up to date with developments. However, at one of his site visits to the pavilion at the end of March 1935 he was clearly delighted with progress, and he wrote to his wife, Louise, from the plane en route to Palestine: "Bexhill on Friday was a great joy. The iron frame is finished and also already a part of the walls. The situation is first class: seen from the sea, the building looks like a horizontal skyscraper which starts its development from the auditorium. Seen from the street, it is a festive invitation. The interior is truly music. Lord De La Warr told me so: he was quite excited."

The walls Mendelsohn witnessed going up were made of reinforced concrete; they were not load-bearing and, as a result, far quicker to erect. The concrete was 10 cm (4 in.) thick, with a mesh of mild steel (steel with little carbon, used for rigidity) rods welded to the frame. Each of the main stanchions, or support girders, of the welded steel frame was encased in concrete (although problems were later to arise with this), and an inner wall of concrete breeze blocks, each 6 cm (2½ in.) thick, was laid and covered with fibreboard to provide an internal finish. Ventilation was provided by a wall cavity that rises through the building, with ventilating tiles around the doors and windows

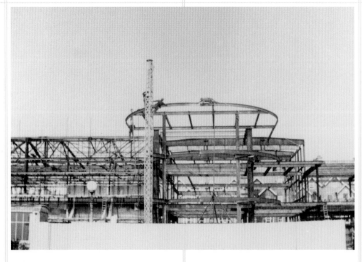

PUTTING ON A GOOD FACE

The external appearance of buildings frequently suggests the atmosphere of the interior. And if only for this reason it is essential for hotels and commercial buildings to take particular care of their exteriors.

Cleveleys Hydro at Blackpool is a case in point. This Hotel, which was previously rendered with an ordinary cement rough cast, was losing some of its inviting looks. Now it has again "put on a good face"—a better face than ever before, in fact, for it has now been rendered with some 43 tons of No. 3 cream "Cullamix," and the result is that the Hydro is now infinitely more attractive.

The old rough cast was hacked off and a backing coat of waterproof cement applied to the brick walls. The finishing coat was then applied and the whole smoothed off with a wood float. This was lightly stippled with a brush.

The plinth was faced with black "Cullamix."

The Architect for this work was Francis L. Lumb, Esq., F.R.I.B.A., of Blackpool, and the Contractors Messrs. J. Tanner & Sons Ltd., of Liverpool.

'Cullamix'

COLOURED PORTLAND CEMENT

Above Earl De La Warr lays the pavilion's foundation plaque, on 6 May 1935.

Above Mixed with mica, the new Cullamix render was designed to glisten in the sunlight.

Left Mendelsohn (pictured sixth from the right in the right-hand image) tours the building site. His rare visits to Bexhill attracted great interest.

Below King George V (wearing hat) and
Queen Mary (front, centre), with Earl De La
Warr (far right), visit Cooden Beach, en
route to the pavilion, in 1935.

Bottom Bexhill's new mayor, Striedlinger
(bowing), and Earl De La Warr greet the
Duke and Duchess of York at the pavilion's
opening ceremony in December 1935.

on each floor, and also by leaving the top of the upper cavity open to the roof space.

Mendelsohn and Chermayeff's original specifications had been to render the outside of the building with a mix containing a bright aggregate such as glass, quartz or mica in the finishing layer, which would sparkle in the sunlight, would resist crazing and would be reasonably self-cleaning in rainstorms. Ultimately, the mix used was ivory-white Cullamix, a proprietary render that offered a suitable, cost-effective solution, and mica. It was laid in sections, in three coats, on consecutive days: water-repellent cement in the first layer, Portland cement in the second, and the final Cullamix layer applied by a hand-operated spatter machine and scraped to the finished texture.

To break up the exterior surfaces of the large auditorium walls, vertical grooves, 25 mm (1 in.) wide and 6 mm (¼ in.) deep, were pressed into the render. The initial effect was unsuccessful, however, as the grooves disappeared when viewed from a distance. Shortly before the building's opening, Mendelsohn ordered that all the strips were to be painted chocolate brown. At this late stage, all the scaffolding around the building had already been removed, and the painting had to be done using a ladder. Just five days before the royal opening, a bucket of brown paint was spilled over the exterior wall, near the building's entrance. Simply painting over the spillage was not possible due to the Cullamix render finish. The scaffolding was hastily brought back, and the exterior panel hacked off, re-rendered and finished. The scaffolding was removed just hours before the royal guests arrived for the grand opening.

With such a complex and pioneering building, it was inevitable that there would be other obstacles along the way. Cost always seemed to play a part. Mendelsohn's original choice of tile for the external columns of the south front and for window and door dressings (and indeed at one time for facing the whole exterior)

had been a faience tile imported from Czechoslovakia. This proved to be too expensive, even for its limited use on the columns and window and door dressings. Instead, British rectangular, pale buff vitreous tiles were used, pointed with a mortar to match their colour. The architects were similarly frustrated in their desire to ensure that the building's exterior metalwork would withstand the rigours of the seaside location (part of the original requirement in the competition design specifications). Aware of the danger of corrosion, they had been in correspondence with the Building Research Station (part of the Ministry of Public Building and Works) as early as February 1934, seeking advice "on any new form of paint or anti-corrosive process before painting steel windows, such as, for example, zinc-spraying". The architects were also interested in the possible use of both bronze and aluminium for the windows and doors, since they also asked whether there was any known method of preventing these materials becoming discoloured, should they be substituted for painted steel.

There is no official record of why the decision was taken to use painted-steel window frames, which were supplied by leading window producer Crittall Manufacturing, but the high cost of the alternatives must have played a part (although there would certainly also have been considerable difficulty obtaining galvanized windows of the size required). However, the initial savings made by the use of painted steel must have been negated many times over in the course of a sixty-year battle against corrosion.

The same victory of cost over build quality appears to have taken place inside the pavilion, but with fewer repercussions. The terrazzo flooring, for example, was specified for a much greater area than it was actually used for, with cork tiles being laid instead almost everywhere apart from the auditorium, where maple strip was used for the sprung dance floor. The terrazzo flooring, where it features, is magnificent. It was laid by a London-based Italian family firm, left to set and then polished with blocks of pumice and other hard stone. The floors could be polished by machine; the stairs, however, required polishing by hand.

By far the greatest victim of the battle over the costs of the pavilion was the loss of the proposal to replace the Edwardian bandstand on the seafront with a circular swimming pool, along with a curved screen and pergola to protect bathers from the onshore breezes. The proposed pool reflected the increasing fashion for healthy, seaside pursuits. Such a trend could be seen particularly along the south coast, where open-air swimming pools had started to spring up, extending the beach inland and lengthening the period during which bathing and outdoor leisure pursuits could be enjoyed.

Although the swimming pool scheme had not been included in the original winning design for the pavilion, by the time of the public inquiry into the project's costs it had become an integral part of the proposals. However, unknown to many in the town hall at the time, the costs of the pool's construction were not included in the designers' estimates, which the original loan sought by the council from the Ministry of Health was intended to cover. As a result, and despite criticisms of the original scheme

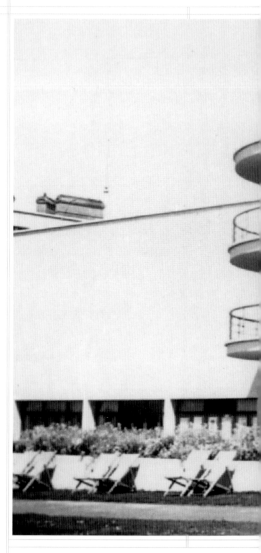

First impressions are important and every visitor to the De La Warr Pavilion is impresse

A beautiful home for the Library, on the upper terrace

e elegant entrance

Spiral staircase connecting the two floors, which is attractive by day and enchanting with lighting effects at night

of the theatre-concert hall, showing the ceiling of many domes which makes it acoustically perfect

Below A section through the north staircase shows the reinforced concrete canopy, first designed as a steel and glazed one.

Bottom A drawing shows the typical external wall construction above the continuous ground-floor windows of the auditorium.

from residents, a second application was made to the ministry, this time for a loan of £18,600 to pay for the construction of the pool connecting the pergola and the pier out to sea.

The ministry itself proved willing to approve the scheme, although it suggested that, in view of the criticisms at the inquiry, the pool's design should be considered further. However, this information was issued by the council in the form of a letter from the town clerk to the chairman of the ratepayers' association, rather than through the more usual channel of providing a full council report. Perhaps angered by what they saw as underhand tactics, objectors to the pavilion's construction were quick to seize on any opportunity to limit its scope. The ratepayers' association was incensed and, at a meeting on 28 October 1935, the local council abandoned the proposal to pursue the swimming pool scheme and decided to defer a decision on the original proposal also to build a pergola on the eastern part of the site. The following month, this, too, was voted out, saving a further £8734.

It had been Mendelsohn's inability to secure commissions, together with concerns about the impending danger to his family's security, that had driven him to England from Nazi Germany, but it was more than the prospect of new work that then drew him so swiftly to Palestine. On visiting the proposed site of Chaim Weizmann's house, Mendelsohn had been inspired by the beauty of the land he had first seen eleven years before, and he spent many hours sketching in the hills near Tel Aviv. Writing from Jerusalem in 1934, he explained: "I am resolved to remain here. Every day I come to regard the people in the fields, even the townspeople, even the European Jews who inhabit the hotel, a little more as my brothers. ... I am absorbed by the work, as in the good old days – England is an interregnum." Certainly, no sooner had he seen construction start on the De La Warr Pavilion than he set his sights elsewhere. Although Mendelsohn still retained his share in the practice in England, by April 1935 he had bought himself out of it for eighteen months, in order to make a fresh start on his own in Palestine.

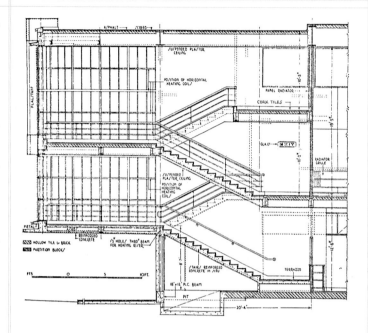

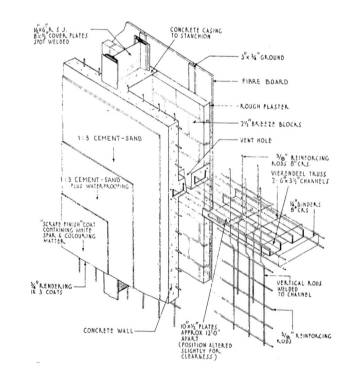

Below A section through the glazed screens
in the restaurant, each 2.4 m (8 ft) wide, shows
the position of the heating panels.

As perhaps the most celebrated Jewish architect of the day, Mendelsohn soon received commissions. Among fellow émigrés to Palestine was his old client Salman Schocken, who intended to build both a new residence in Jerusalem and a library for his priceless collection of rare books and prints. Mendelsohn's commissions – the Hadassah University Medical Centre, the Anglo-Palestinian Bank Building, both in Jerusalem – got progressively bigger, demanding more time and energy, and making managing an office in both London and Jerusalem increasingly difficult.

The real reasons for the split between Mendelsohn and Chermayeff are not well documented but appear to be a mix of clashes over professional integrity and money. In *Erich Mendelsohn: The Complete Works* (1999), Bruno Zevi reports Louise Mendelsohn's record of the dispute that arose after one of her husband's visits to Jerusalem: "When he returned, many reasons for disagreement came to light on account of the details of the buildings as they were carried out. It appeared clear that the partnership could not continue" (p. 207). Mendelsohn thought that Chermayeff was interfering; Chermayeff was in turn angered by Mendelsohn's decision to set up his own practice in Palestine while still demanding a share of the profits from the London office. Chermayeff recalled in an interview with Richard Plunz in 1980: "We really quarrelled. I thought he was being greedy and that immediately finished it" (Plunz 1982). For Mendelsohn, a new start in Palestine was the only option. Three days after the tour of the pavilion with Earl De La Warr in March 1935 he was back on a plane to Jerusalem. He wrote to his wife: "Under the impression of this apparently successful beginning the final agreement with Serge came about. We parted fully reconciled and in the awareness that each had found his mark and sphere of activity." The designs perfected, the working drawings complete, construction under way and a trusted team of architects and engineers in place to oversee it, Mendelsohn was clearly satisfied that his tasks were done. It was up to Chermayeff to finish the job.

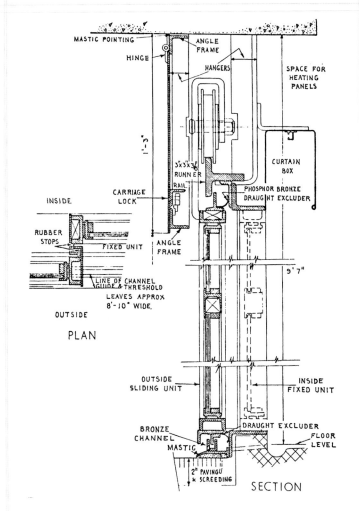

PLAN

SECTION

chapter 4   a race against time

The changes that had been made to the pavilion design during Mendelsohn's absence are not recorded, but changes there definitely were. The principal alterations were made to the entertainments hall. In the original design, the central staircases projected almost a full storey higher than the auditorium, which was itself only slightly taller than the restaurant wing. The staircases provided the vertical axis favoured by Mendelsohn to balance the longer, horizontal plane of the building. In addition, there was a row of windows running along the top of the auditorium, continuing the horizontal lines of the restaurant and reading-room terraces and breaking up what would otherwise have been a large mass of wall.

By the time the model was produced in April 1934, however, the auditorium had increased substantially in size, and a line of French windows had been placed along the south wall, opening out on to a separate terrace not unlike the competition design put forward by Haswell and Shepherd. The west wing, in other words, had become a much larger and rather uniform block, the form of which was further emphasized by the addition of a projection on the roof to house some of the ventilation outlets for the air conditioning.

The alterations had been made for practical reasons, however, resulting from the council's decision that the pavilion should have a properly equipped stage. Although this had not been specified in the design brief, it was clear the building would require a much deeper stage area than had originally been envisaged, to accommodate the required equipment. The architects did their best to make the necessary alterations, but there were immediate knock-on effects. The increased size of the auditorium, which still needed to accommodate 1500 people, made the seating plan much flatter in shape, and added more depth to the gallery, thus requiring the gallery's seating to be raised to provide the rake necessary to see the stage. Raising the seating, in turn, blocked a row of air intakes for the air conditioning; the remaining row of outlets therefore had to work much faster, resulting in noise and draughts. The full impact of the changes was not discovered until after the building opened. Until the problem was resolved, the entire air-conditioning system had to be shut off during performances.

The French windows were also problematic. Strong sunlight overheated the hall in the summer, so heavy curtains were used to block out the light (and to insulate the room in the winter), but their deadening effect caused problems with the auditorium acoustics. These were only partially resolved once the building had opened by covering the auditorium walls with sound-reflecting paint. The increased size of the auditorium meant that the hall now rose up to meet the full height of the building, the top storey of which, in the original design, had included only a covered walkway and viewing platform. This concept was consequently scrapped, and the conference (or lecture) room was extended upwards from the first floor to occupy part of the top storey, enabling natural light to enter the room from windows at the upper level on the east. This alteration, however, meant that the initial proposal for a projecting rest room, originally designed to cantilever out together with the north staircase, was also abandoned. To some critics, this was a detrimental step: the original projection had been designed to display posters and illuminated signs advertising the pavilion's events. Its subsequent replacement with a board for brash paper posters attracted criticism from the architectural firm of Connell, Ward & Lucas, which, shortly after the building's opening, wrote to the *Bexhill-on-Sea Observer* lamenting that, as a result of the use of the board, this "most successful attempt to provide good architecture on the coast" was "well on the way to being spoiled through general lack of imagination, good sense and good taste" (11 January 1936, p.11).

Although these alterations to the original design proved troublesome, they did not substantially affect the overall plan and concept. Greater changes were made, however, to the building's landscaping. Prior to the architects' proposals that the bandstand should be transformed into a circular swimming pool, Mendelsohn's drawings for both the north and south terraces included distinct, vertical points to punctuate what was otherwise a building with a strong horizontal composition. To the north, Mendelsohn proposed a number of flagpoles from which would be flown the town's coat of arms, among other motifs. To the south, there was to be a large statue of Persephone at the apex of the sweeping seaward lawns.

Below By the time the building was complete, the band of windows proposed for the upper part of the auditorium wing had disappeared.

Bottom, left Frank Dobson (1886–1963) was commissioned to produce a dramatic statue for the south terrace. It was never finished, but this maquette survives.

Bottom, right The first floor provided a bright, airy lecture theatre with flexible, stackable seating – the perfect place to display Dobson's maquette of Persephone.

Above The architects' dream of
contrasting vertical and horizontal
axes is finally realized.

Below A ticket office nestles neatly at the foot of the north staircase.

Bottom The entrance hall leads gracefully into a spacious auditorium foyer.

Mendelsohn had long been an enthusiast for the use of sculpture within his architectural designs, and his vision of Persephone, Greek goddess of the underworld, gazing out to sea towards France as his original drawings suggested, could refer to his much-vaunted plans for a European Academy of the Mediterranean. A number of eminent sculptors were invited to put forward designs for the sculpture, including the eventual winner, Frank Dobson, later to become an official war artist during the Second World War and professor of sculpture at the Royal College of Art from 1946 to 1953.

Mendelsohn himself was in correspondence with a number of artists prior to Dobson's commission, which suggests that he took a particular interest in this feature of the overall scheme. However, having attacked the proposed swimming pool scheme over its cost, the local ratepayers' association swiftly turned its attention towards the statue. Defiantly, the editor of the *Bexhill-on-Sea Observer* spoke out: "I hope nobody will run away with the idea that the proposal to embellish the Marina Hall [the name by which the pavilion was known before its opening] with a statue is an afterthought which will add another £500 to the cost. The statue is not an 'extra'. It was provided for in the plans and included in the estimate, and if this is the first the public has heard about it, it may be owing to the inability of the layman to understand architects' drawings" (2 February 1935, p. 2). The statue had also featured in the model of the building displayed prominently at the public inquiry into the pavilion's costs.

Once commissioned, Dobson started work on the piece, which was to have stood 5.2 m (17 ft) high. A maquette is now in the National Museum and Gallery of Wales, in Cardiff, but the sculpture itself was never executed. The abandonment of the swimming pool and pier proposal, the objections to the erection of a raised pergola screen, the cancellation of the statue – all were driven by the constant effort to reduce the burden of the project's costs on the local ratepayers. Philistinism played its part, too. Two months before the pavilion's opening, the council agreed to defer consideration of the statue until after the building's completion, amid claims from councillors that "a statue of such

Below The only artwork eventually included in the finished design, Edward Wadsworth's mural originally graced the end of the restaurant wing. Also pictured are the colourful chairs and tables designed by Alvar Aalto, which made the cafeteria a bright and busy place.

Left A perspective sketch shows the dramatic lines of the auditorium. Chermayeff is largely credited with the design of the pavilion's interior fittings.

Below Panelled bookcases with light veneer maintained the air of modernity throughout the building.

Left Wadsworth created only the original study for the mural, illustrated here. The final, full-scale version was eventually realized by his assistant.

a nature would make the council the laughing stock of the whole town", and that the £900 allocated to pay for it would be "a wicked waste of money". The critics had claimed yet another victim in Mendelsohn and Chermayeff's original vision for the pavilion. Like the goddess it was intended to represent, Dobson's Persephone was condemned to the infernal regions.

Although there had been alterations, cost-cutting and curtailments, the fundamental scheme for the pavilion was still intact and, once left alone, the result was of the highest quality. The revamped design of the entertainments hall, with removable seating, meant that it could be used for a variety of purposes and the floor could be cleared for dances and balls. The doors leading into the auditorium were also designed to be retractable, opening out the auditorium into the foyer to create a larger space.

Frank Birch and Edgar Jackson were employed to act as theatre consultants in the stage and lighting design. Birch recalled in 1936: "We were asked to advise on and equip a modern theatre, suitable for all purposes, conventional and otherwise, and to keep in mind the fact that the hall, which was the theatre, could also be used for other than theatrical entertainments. It is true that expenses were cut down and our scheme had to be considerably modified, but it is nonetheless true that the Bexhill stage can be conveniently used for every type of drama and for every technique of production and presentation. And to that extent it is unique" (*Architectural Review*, vol. 80, July 1936, p. 20). In addition to dwindling budgets, the theatre designers faced other, more prosaic obstacles. Writing in 1991 at the age of eighty-four, Jackson recalled: "My recollection of [Mendelsohn] is of a vague but enthusiastic fellow frightfully keen on getting things done quickly without much talk. My memory of Bexhill in the 1930s is more vivid. When we visited the job in July the work was held up as all the concreters there became ice-cream men in the summer!" (letter to Jill Theis, 8 March 1991, De La Warr Pavilion Archive).

Despite the financial costs and the demands of the British summer, by the autumn of 1935 most of the important elements of the original Mendelsohn and Chermayeff plan had been installed.

While a little more solid than originally expected, the cantilevered system of construction had worked well, and the terraces and balconies appeared sleek and slender. The layout of the interior was working perfectly, with the balconies providing shade from the harsh summer light while also allowing natural light deep into the building during the winter months, ideal for the pavilion's light, bright reading room. Inside, the building could not have contrasted more starkly with the former fashion for municipal architecture. The heavy wooden panelling of Edwardian council offices (and even those designed in a more avant-garde, Arts and Crafts style) had been swept away in favour of cream plastered walls that were contrasted, in certain areas, with entire walls painted powder blue or light green.

The colours of the interior were reflected in the choice of furniture. In the reading room, for example, Chermayeff installed a collection of PLAN chairs upholstered in pale blue. In the cafeteria and restaurant he opted for more sturdy furniture, yet even there everything had a modern look. There was no heavy oak or mahogany to be seen; diners were instead treated to contemporary Finmar bentwood chairs and tables of natural, light beech designed by the renowned Finnish architect and designer Alvar Aalto, their brightly coloured seats and surfaces painted vermilion and pale blue – colours scarcely seen in furniture at the time. The combination of PLAN and Aalto furniture had already been used by the architect Oliver Hill in a mock-up of an apartment interior for Berthold Lubetkin's new Highpoint I housing development in Highgate, north London, which was displayed at the 1934 exhibition *Contemporary Industrial Design in the Home* at Dorland Hall on Regent Street. Lubetkin had been so impressed by the arrangement that he had the entire interior transferred directly to his own apartment at Highpoint. Chermayeff, who had organized a similar exhibition at Whiteleys store in west London a year before, was quick to spot what would work in his new pavilion. Everything was open-plan: there were no cloths to cover unsightly table legs, no drawers beneath tables or desks; even the armchairs had tubular steel supports to let the light pass through. For a building with such forward-looking architecture, it was only fitting that its interior was at the cutting edge of new design.

Below The original colour scheme for the pavilion auditorium used an array of tones unusual for that time.

Bottom, left Mendelsohn first used his spiral light fitting in the German Metalworkers' Union building in Berlin (1929–30).

Bottom, right Both the staircase and the light fitting in the Berlin building were near identical to those designed for Bexhill.

Chermayeff was also responsible for commissioning the pavilion's famous mural at the end of the restaurant from Edward Wadsworth, a former member of the Vorticist movement, the British avant-garde group of artists associated with the Futurists and Cubists. Wadsworth was a close friend of Chermayeff and frequently invited him to his house in Maresfield, East Sussex, only a few miles from Bexhill. Although Wadsworth produced the original sketch, he was unable to finish the work himself after being commissioned by the Cunard company to design a series of murals for the *Queen Mary* ocean liner. He left the mural's completion to Charles Howard, a young American artist whom Chermayeff had proposed for the task. Wadsworth generously covered the costs of the mural himself.

Although Wadsworth's mural was the only decorative art in the pavilion, colour filled the interior. The restaurant's north wall was painted pale turquoise, lightly toning with the cork-tiled floor, which had a sprung maple dance floor at the end capable of holding eighty couples. In the auditorium, the bright white ceiling was complemented by off-white walls and the rich Australian walnut plywood panelling at ground-floor level. The carpet was dark brown, as were the side curtains, but the proscenium curtains were made of pale blue satin, contrasting with the dark blue upholstery of the stalls seating.

A different range of PLAN chairs was used in the lounge, but these were also upholstered in blue, while the partition between the lounge and the servery and bar was in the same powder blue as the reading-room seats. Even the staff uniforms were colourful: the pavilion attendants wore airforce-blue outfits trimmed with gold braid, the firemen had more conventional uniforms but with red piping down the sides of the trousers, while the two car-park attendants had double-breasted brown jackets with breeches and leggings. All had matching hats with the words 'De La Warr Pavilion' proudly emblazoned on the front.

The reading room was tranquility itself, with cream walls and ceiling, free-standing bookshelves in bays, smokers' tables and comfortable armchairs. The library was particularly important to

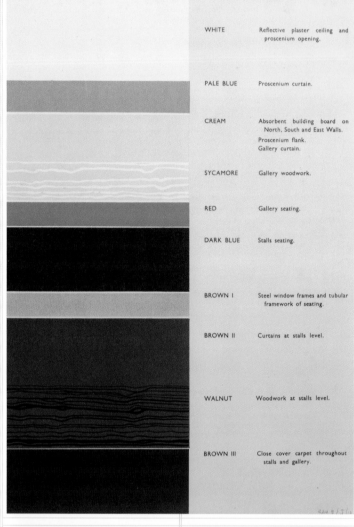

WHITE	Reflective plaster ceiling and proscenium opening.
PALE BLUE	Proscenium curtain.
CREAM	Absorbent building board on North, South and East Walls. Proscenium flank. Gallery curtain.
SYCAMORE	Gallery woodwork.
RED	Gallery seating.
DARK BLUE	Stalls seating.
BROWN I	Steel window frames and tubular framework of seating.
BROWN II	Curtains at stalls level.
WALNUT	Woodwork at stalls level.
BROWN III	Close cover carpet throughout stalls and gallery.

Earl De La Warr since it, together with plans for the entertainments programme and the health-giving aspects of the building's sun parlour, added considerably to the aim of enlightenment that characterized socialist principles. Work towards creating a library in the town had started as early as 1924, but it was not until the opening of the pavilion that it found a proper home. In June 1936 some 3000 books were transferred to the pavilion, together with a regular supply of newspapers and periodicals.

The fixtures and fittings were also of the highest quality. Mendelsohn's signature curving staircase, encased in glass on the south terrace, was fitted with anodized steel handrails, while a long, pendulous steel and chrome lamp, modelled on his previous design for the German Metalworkers' Union building in Berlin, was suspended down its full length. Garrard provided clocks; Mappin & Webb produced the silver cutlery and flower vases engraved with the name of the pavilion; and Troughton & Young the globe electric light fittings that hung from every ceiling. The cafeteria's kitchen, which ran the full length of the restaurant, was fitted out by Benham & Sons with Prestcold refrigerators and a Kelvinator ice-cream machine.

Attention to detail extended to the exterior, too. In keeping with the building's theme of lines, curves and circles, three signs were commissioned to announce the pavilion's name: a large, circular one for the west end of the south, auditorium wall; a second to be placed on the east wall; and a third to run horizontally across the main entrance to the building, characteristic of the style that Mendelsohn had used previously for his Schocken department stores in Stuttgart and Chemnitz. Debate continues as to which of the pavilion's signs were originally neon-lit. Certainly, the sign on the eastern wall was electrified, and there are photographs in which the sign on the south wall is also illuminated. Economy may have led to the decision not to illuminate the front main entrance sign in neon. In all, the signs cost £340, which the council decided to pay for on hire-purchase at a rate of £9 10s. a month.

Eleven months after the coastguard cottages had been demolished, the pavilion was nearing completion. Designs had been altered,

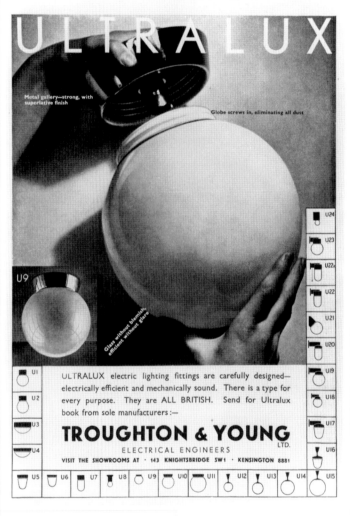

THE ARCHITECTS' JOURNAL for July 11, 1935   xxix

ULTRALUX

Metal gallery—strong, with superlative finish

Globe screws in, eliminating all dust

Glass without blemish, efficient without glare

ULTRALUX electric lighting fittings are carefully designed—electrically efficient and mechanically sound. There is a type for every purpose. They are ALL BRITISH. Send for Ultralux book from sole manufacturers:—

TROUGHTON & YOUNG LTD.

ELECTRICAL ENGINEERS

VISIT THE SHOWROOMS AT · 143 KNIGHTSBRIDGE SW1 · KENSINGTON 8881

Left As in the Berlin building, Bexhill's sweeping staircase formed the focal point of the interior.

Below An original poster shows the range of entertainment on offer right from the opening day of the pavilion, in December 1935.

Bottom The Duke and Duchess of York pose on the stairs before taking their tour of the building on opening day.

new construction techniques introduced, projects cancelled and a seemingly endless battery of questions answered by councillors, clerks, architects and builders. But while progress had been swift, with the interior being decked out in its bright colours and the exterior gleaming in the sunshine in its coat of Cullamix, meeting the final opening deadline, fixed firmly in the royal diary of the Duke and Duchess of York, was a challenge. Indeed, considerable work was still being carried out on the building until the last minute, as Pavilion Trust founder Peter Evenden recalled:

It was 11 December, the day before the grand opening. As evening fell, the south terrace of the pavilion was floodlit all night long. I thought it interesting – if a little late – but it wasn't for artistic effect. In fact, the lights were there for what seemed like an army of men laying the paving on the south terrace in time for the opening. I have no idea how they did it in time – it's a large area. Nonetheless, by the morning, the terrace was complete.

('The Story of Bexhill and the De La Warr Pavilion' 1999)

For the visiting royals, 12 December 1935 started quietly. The Duke and Duchess of York (who became George VI and Queen Elizabeth on the abdication of Edward VIII a year later) arrived on a scheduled train from London and alighted at Cooden Beach. They walked, with little ceremony, the few hundred metres down the road to the De La Warrs' hotel for lunch. It was, according to Cyril Sweett, "a rather wet and blustery day and she [the duchess] complained at having been kept waiting at Cooden Station, which I am afraid made her less than happy for the rest of the day" (*Erich Mendelsohn 1887–1953* 1987, p. 69). Nevertheless, only a few hours later, their trip was transformed into one with the full pomp and ceremony of an official royal visit, with streets packed with onlookers and official guests. A team from Pathé News was there to record the event so it could be broadcast in newsreels around the country.

Initially, all went well. The royal couple were presented to the hundreds of invited guests, and then speeches ensued. In his official address, even Earl De La Warr's recent successor as mayor

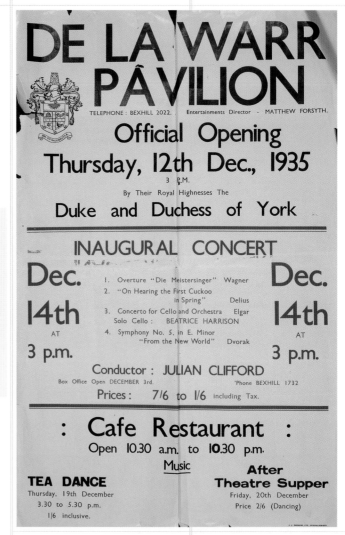

DE LA WARR
PÂVILION

TELEPHONE : BEXHILL 2022.   Entertainments Director - MATTHEW FORSYTH.

Official Opening
Thursday, 12th Dec., 1935
3 P.M.

By Their Royal Highnesses The

Duke and Duchess of York

INAUGURAL CONCERT

Dec.
14th
AT
3 p.m.

1. Overture "Die Meistersinger" Wagner
2. "On Hearing the First Cuckoo
   in Spring"   Delius
3. Concerto for Cello and Orchestra Elgar
   Solo Cello : BEATRICE HARRISON
4. Symphony No. 5, in E. Minor
   "From the New World"   Dvorak

Dec.
14th
AT
3 p.m.

Conductor : JULIAN CLIFFORD
Box Office Open DECEMBER 3rd.   'Phone BEXHILL 1732
Prices :   7/6 to 1/6 including Tax.

: Cafe Restaurant :
Open 10.30 a.m. to 10.30 p.m.
Music

TEA DANCE
Thursday, 19th December
3.30 to 5.30 p.m.
1/6 inclusive.

After
Theatre Supper
Friday, 20th December
Price 2/6 (Dancing)

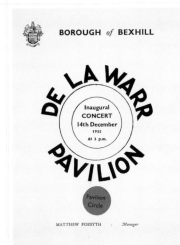

BOROUGH *of* BEXHILL

DE LA WARR PAVILION

Inaugural
CONCERT
14th December
1935
At 3 p.m.

Pavilion
Circle

MATTHEW FORSYTH : *Manager*

of Bexhill, Alderman Colonel O. Striedlinger (who had long been an opponent of the scheme) was forced to admit that the pavilion "strikes a new and original note in buildings of its kind in the country, and represents the last word in the scientific employment of modern building materials and methods of construction" (*Bexhill-on-Sea Observer*, 14 December 1935, p.1). A sudden noise, sounding like heavy rain on the ceiling of the auditorium, then interrupted the speeches. A team was dispatched to investigate. They soon discovered that the noise came not from rain, but from condensation pouring down on to the ceiling from the roof sheeting. After a cold night with a clear sky, the uprush of warm air from the packed auditorium, humidified by the air-conditioning plant as well as the audience, had caused a sudden and very heavy precipitation that was threatening the audience below.

Worse was to come. During his investigation the clerk of works put a foot through the saturated ceiling. It was an assistant, Ken Rome, who saved the day, spending most of the remaining two and a half hours holding back the damaged ceiling panel with wire, arms aching while patiently listening to the muffled speeches, concert and applause taking place down below. Unaware that the ceiling might be about to cave in on top of the audience, the Duke of York continued the proceedings with a brief speech. Judging by its paternalistic tone, it could have been written by Earl De La Warr himself: "Looking into the future, it appears to me that, owing to man's greater efficiency and the advent of machinery and other inventions, an increase in leisure is coming to the people of this country, and it will be well to suggest to people how to amuse themselves when not at work. This great pavilion of yours will certainly give suggestions to those of future generations in methods for employing their leisure."

Declaring the building open, the duke then pressed a button on top of a model of a silver Martello tower. (Martello towers were the circular coastal fortresses built during the Napoleonic wars, one of which had stood on the pavilion site until it was demolished in 1870.) With that, the stage curtains drew back to reveal the pavilion symphony orchestra, which, under the conductorship of the new musical director, Julian Clifford, immediately struck up the tune *Sussex by the Sea*, a fitting overture that heralded further pieces by Elgar, Liszt, Rossini and Mendelssohn's own favourite, Bach.

The concert over, the royal party left the auditorium to tour the building before the public was let into the pavilion for the first time. Remembering that his assistant was still stranded in the roof space, the clerk of works returned to inform him that all had gone well and he could return to his other duties. With that the assistant let go of the wire, and the entire ceiling panel crashed 15 m (50 ft) to the floor, directly on to the seating area where the royal couple and other guests had been only twenty minutes before.

chapter 5   the pavilion in its prime

From the moment the De La Warr Pavilion opened on 12 December 1935, praise was heaped on the building's design and construction techniques, and also on the town that had so boldly sponsored its development. The formal opening received wide coverage in the national press, with *The Times* sending a special correspondent to the inauguration, and the *London Evening Standard* running a special edition that went on sale that same afternoon in the town. Although the Duchess of York had reportedly been in a bad mood at the opening, the *Bexhill-on-Sea Observer* headline that week read "Enchanting Smiles of Popular Duchess" (14 December 1935, p.1), and the newspaper carried a full-length illustrated report. The playwright George Bernard Shaw sent a postcard of congratulation to Matthew Forsyth, the pavilion's new entertainments director, which was reproduced in the opening programme. "Delighted to hear that Bexhill has emerged from barbarism at last", Shaw wrote, adding that he would refrain from giving the place "a clean bill of civilisation until all my plays are performed there once a year at least".

On the opening day, *The Architects' Journal* ran an extensive illustrated article on the building, with a full analysis of its plans and construction techniques. In the following weeks, further articles appeared, providing more detailed plans and section drawings, in *The Architects' Journal*, *Architect and Building News*, *The Builder* and many other periodicals, demonstrating how highly the architectural press rated the building's innovations and technical mastery.

The Times was fulsome in its praise: "It is difficult to know which to congratulate most – the designers, Dr Erich Mendelsohn and Mr Serge Chermayeff; the assessor who selected the design from an open competition in 1934; or the Bexhill Corporation. It is by far the most civilised thing that has been done on the South Coast since the days of the Regency, of which it may fairly be said to continue the tradition in contemporary terms" (14 December 1935, p.14).

Opposite From the moment it opened in 1935 (bottom left), the pavilion was thronged with visitors day and night.

Below The north exterior of the new pavilion proclaimed the name of its founder in bold lettering.

Bottom Ample parking provision, seen in this view from the east, meant that the building was originally surrounded by open space.

Charles Reilly, the Liverpool professor of architecture who had championed Mendelsohn when he first arrived in Britain in a series of lectures, paid him due credit in the *Manchester Guardian*:

When the award of the assessor, Mr T.S. Tait, himself a leading modernist, was announced and it was found that the winning design was by the famous German architect Erich Mendelsohn and his English partner, Serge Chermayeff, it became a matter of general interest for everyone that we should be about to have in this country a first-class building with the name of the chief leader of the modern movement attached to it. Now that the building is finished it is possible to see how much we have been enriched by receiving into our midst once again a leader of thought rejected by his own country.

It is safe to say that no such simple and elegant structure, none so novel in its straightforwardness and efficiency, has before been put up here as a pleasure pavilion. When one looks at the plain cream surfaces, divided by the long vertical lines, to define the inevitable graduations in colour, one wonders whether we are yet ready, and particularly whether Bexhill is yet ready, for such elegance.

(13 December 1935)

Reilly's words were strangely prescient. Despite the praise bestowed on the building by the nation's architects and critics, the angry and highly vocal minority who had so affected the pavilion's progress thus far could not be kept quiet. On the day of the pavilion's opening, the *Daily Mirror* published an article airing the opinions of Bexhill's residents. Referring perhaps to the proposed Dobson statue, but taken to relate to the entire enterprise, one resident, Sir Duncombe Mann, said: "I am no admirer of this Epstein stuff" (12 December 1935). Earlier that year there had been renewed moral outrage at Jacob Epstein's Modernist sculptures of naked figures on the former British Medical Association building on the Strand in central London.

Although acclaim for the building's design was by no means widespread among the locals, there was little that opponents could do about it: the pavilion stood defiant, a triumph of the new over the old. However mutterings immediately began over the

Below Julian Clifford, the pavilion's first musical director, was already well known, and brought immediate prestige.

Bottom The much-photographed pavilion became a popular subject for the local postcard manufacturer Judges.

direction of the pavilion's entertainments policy, with the *Bexhill-on-Sea Observer* reporting of the inaugural concert: "While little fault was found with its presentation, there was a general complaint that it was an unsuitable choice for such an occasion and a lighter note would have met the wishes of the majority of the audience" (14 December 1935, p. 1). It was only a short time before the same arguments that had simmered for so long over the cost of the building's construction focused on this new line of attack.

In the hope of attracting regular visitors of a 'theatre and concert circle', the pavilion had been launched with a new concept, offering local ratepayers – as stakeholders in the new enterprise – reductions in admission prices to musical and other performances. By buying a book of vouchers in advance, circle members could obtain a reduction in the price of any ticket they purchased. The launch of the offer had proved successful, with more than 1000 books of vouchers being sold prior to the building's opening.

The entertainments policy was initially seen as something of an experiment, and was structured to appeal to people of all tastes through different types of performance. The first play presented at the pavilion, *Viceroy Sarah*, had a London cast headed by the leading actress Violet Farebrother, while the first production by the Bexhill Amateur Theatrical Society (BATS), in April 1936, was the comedy thriller *Road House*. The society, which produced numerous plays at the pavilion over the years, had been formed in 1935 under the presidency of Countess De La Warr and the chairmanship of one of Bexhill's residents, Major Ronald Cargill.

The musical director, Julian Clifford, was a leading conductor, a former Hastings resident who, as well as conducting many of the principal orchestras of the day, had previously been one of only three conductors engaged in 1930 by the Royal Philharmonic Society, alongside Sir Thomas Beecham and Sir Henry Wood. His appointment, in which Earl De La Warr had played a key role, had been a wise choice. Clifford helped give Bexhill much of the prestige enjoyed by competing seaside towns, with his regular broadcasts with the BBC Symphony Orchestra effectively acting as national adverts for the new entertainments attraction.

SUNDAY, FEBRUARY 9th, at 3 p.m.

SYMPHONY CONCERT

The Pavilion Orchestra
(Augmented)

Conductor:
JULIAN CLIFFORD

1. CONCERTO GROSSO No. 10 FOR STRINGS ... ... *Handel*
2. SIEGFRIED IDYLL ... ... *Wagner*
3. CONCERTO IN D MINOR FOR PIANO AND ORCHESTRA *Mozart*
    Solo Piano - WALTER COLLINS
4. SYMPHONY No. 101—" The Clock" ... ... *Haydn*

PRICES - 3/-, 2/-, 1/6, 1/- (including tax). All Bookable

THE DE LA WARR PAVILION, BEXHILL-ON-SEA

Below Matthew Forsyth (top), entertainments director at the pavilion, cleverly mixed top-name acts with local productions by, for example, the Bexhill Amateur Theatrical Society (BATS).

Despite the renown and reputation of the pavilion's two directors, Forsyth for entertainments and Clifford for music, the initial experiment to cater for both high-culture and popular-culture audiences quickly attracted criticism. Musically, the aim had been to provide a varied programme of symphony concerts, chamber music, celebrity recitals and lighter musical concerts in the main auditorium, with trios and quartets playing light music for coffee mornings or tea dances in the afternoons in the café. Nine musicians had been recruited to form the basis of a permanent orchestra, which could be expanded as required, with the eventual aim of developing, over time, a first-class orchestra to compare with any other in the provinces. By March 1936, however, not four months after the pavilion's opening, the criticisms had begun. Debate raged in the *Bexhill-on-Sea Observer* over what the musical director had meant when he explained that the entertainments policy would appeal to both "high" and "low" brows. Criticism was levelled at the poor attendance of "high-brow" classical concerts, which, some believed, were being subsidized by the higher attendances enjoyed by the pavilion's lighter popular concerts and plays. The arguments took off: some residents were offended at being called "low-brow", while others simply attacked the events put on at the pavilion as mere "rubbish", stating that they continued to travel to Hastings, with its variety shows and dance halls, for their enjoyment.

In a bid to obtain more considered feedback on the programme, the directors had conducted a survey of the pavilion circle members, asking them about their preferences for the entertainments provided. The findings made gloomy reading. At a packed meeting of nearly eight hundred members of the circle in March, the directors were put to the test, fielding a series of questions on the survey. The chairman of the council's entertainments committee, Councillor W.N. Cuthbert, also attended. Most people who had taken part in the survey preferred the main auditorium to be run as a theatre, with the majority expressing a preference for touring company productions over those of the resident repertory company. Yet while the touring 'try-outs' for London theatres had been successful, they were not always possible to stage at late notice, and more regular

The Staff of the De La Warr Pavilion feel it a great honour to be entrusted with the task of controlling the future career of the Pavilion, and are determined to maintain the highest possible standard in keeping with its architectural distinctions.

They are all entirely at the service of Bexhill and all future patrons of Bexhill.

Matthew Forsyth

Entertainments and Publicity Manager: EDMUND RHODES.
Box Office Manager: W. HATCHARD. *London Press Representative*: DAVID EVANS.
Stage Manager: J. CARTER. *Chief Engineer*: L. STEEN.
Licensee: **MATTHEW FORSYTH,** *Entertainments Director*

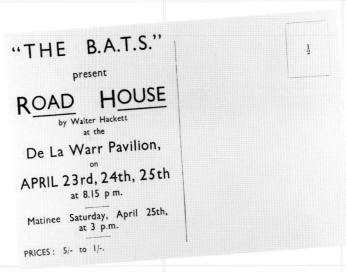

"THE B.A.T.S."
present
ROAD HOUSE
by Walter Hackett
at the
De La Warr Pavilion,
on
APRIL 23rd, 24th, 25th
at 8.15 p.m.

Matinee Saturday, April 25th, at 3 p.m.

PRICES: 5/- to 1/-.

bookings were needed to maintain revenue. Perhaps not surprisingly, it had been the celebrity concerts and shows that had proved most popular. In the first few months after its opening, the pavilion played host to such luminaries as Dame Sybil Thorndike, Paul Robeson and Fritz Kreisler, the leading violinist of his day. The members of the circle also preferred the programme's lighter, popular music concerts over the efforts to develop classical music at the pavilion, although the numbers supporting symphony concerts were greatly in excess of those favouring the new forms of jazz or dance music.

The meeting proved to be more than simply an opportunity for feedback, although there were many who spoke out in favour of the pavilion's clearly excellent programme. After listening to the presentations and debates, Councillor Cuthbert surprised onlookers – chiefly the two pavilion directors – by announcing that the entertainments committee had decided that, regretfully, it would cut the pavilion's programme of symphony concerts, finding they were "spending £110 and taking £17 on the gate". Protesting that the councillor had taken the lowest figure for any takings and the highest figure for expenditure, an appalled Julian Clifford forcefully argued for the programme to be maintained: "We cannot work up symphony concerts in three months. No one else has done it and I do not see why we should be expected to do it here." To general applause, he added: "It took my father [also a conductor] three years to create a public for good music at Hastings." But the decision had been taken: in a year of "unusual" expenditure, the councillor said, the council had to put its finger on the biggest loss. Just three months into the pavilion's life, one of its main functions – to enlighten and educate the population through a sophisticated and varied programme of entertainment – had been confined to the dustbin. Bowing to pressure from ratepayers, and completely disregarding the circle members' opinions, the 'old guard' wanted revenge. The "low-brow" campaigners were winning the argument.

Worse was to follow. In April 1936, the council announced the new rate to be levied in the town. The rate was to rise by 1s. 6d. in the pound for the year 1936–37, most of it attributable to increases in the rate levied for entertainments. Uproar ensued, and the local ratepayers' association laid the blame on the costs of the new pavilion. The association accused the council of going back on promises to safeguard against scandalous rate increases to pay for the pavilion's running costs. It called for a new inquiry to be instigated by the district auditor to ascertain whether all the loan monies provided to the council had been used correctly. The argument spilled over into the local newspaper, sparking a new round of furious accusations from residents that the council had acted improperly. "Squandermania", ran the headlines. Yet despite the fact that the pavilion was still running at a deficit – £8799 by the end of the financial year – there was distinct evidence that its fortunes were, in fact, turning around, and losses were diminishing. Furthermore, after scouring hundreds of pages of expenditure accounts provided by the architects, the auditor only disallowed a payment of £44 made to them by the council, and took the unusual step of congratulating the corporation on the actual care and attention that had been given to protecting its interests in carrying out the work. The *Bexhill-on-Sea Observer* commented that, in a contract of £70,000, it was "an exceedingly small mouse for the mountain of investigation to produce" (7 October 1967, p. 21).

Another casualty emerged from the furore. Earl De La Warr had lost his mayoralty in elections held only one month before the opening of the pavilion, in November 1935. However, in recognition of his mayoralty being "the principal factor in carrying through the scheme to a successful conclusion", the building was named after him shortly before its completion. Now the council wished to honour the former mayor – by now president of the Board of Education and a leading light in the cabinet – further by offering him the freedom of the borough. But the years of anger and accusation had taken their toll. De La Warr diplomatically turned down the council's offer, stating: "It would naturally be pleasing to receive such an honour, feeling that it was with the approval of the burgesses of Bexhill, but while so much controversy about the pavilion still exists, there would evidently be a certain number who would once again condemn the action of the council" (*Bexhill-on-Sea Observer*, 27 June 1936, p. 1).

Below By day the sun cast myriad shadows throughout the building, accentuating its lines. The building's original signage can also be seen in this photograph.

Below In contrast, by night the building's lines were dramatically picked out by electric light against the darkness.

Pages 102–103 Outdoor displays, such as this hoop-and-ball show sponsored by the *Daily Mirror*, brought spectators to the pavilion in their droves.

Below, top The pavilion roof played host to outdoor games such as quoits.

Below, centre George Bernard Shaw's play *The Millionairess* premiered at the pavilion in 1936.

Although there were clearly some critics who remained opposed to Bexhill's new attraction, its popularity with visitors was undeniable. The building was frequently packed at weekends, and the mix of touring company performances and pre-London theatre 'try-outs', and the burgeoning reputation of its repertory company, the Forsyth Players, were attracting large audiences.

By 1936 the newly electrified line of the Southern Railway was bringing thousands of new visitors to the coast on its Sunny South Express train, and the pavilion featured in dramatic new railway posters extolling the virtues of sunshine, health and entertainment. In line with this image, the pavilion sought to stage such events as the *Daily Mirror* hoop-and-ball competitions. Badminton and quoits were played on the roof terrace, and whist drives, bridge tournaments, piano competitions, gymnasium displays and exhibitions took place in the auditorium. All these activities brought in a new range of visitors, both local and from further afield.

With its new lecture theatre and auditorium, the pavilion started to attract the attention of the country's growing conference circuit, too, with the Design and Industries Association holding its first-ever conference at the pavilion in 1937, only two months after the prime minister, Neville Chamberlain, and his wife had visited the town's new attraction. Lectures also proved very popular. William Wedgwood Benn, the former secretary of state for India, opened the lecture programme with a survey of the state of the world in 1935, while other speakers included such luminaries as the broadcaster Sir Frederick Whyte and Everest explorer Frank Smythe.

The early financial losses at the pavilion, and the subsequent decision by the council to curtail some of the programme and let the main hall for an autumn repertory season, led Matthew Forsyth to resign his position as entertainments director. He focused instead on building up the reputation of the Forsyth Players, his repertory company, and on developing the pavilion into the county theatre for East Sussex.

For some years, plays would be staged throughout the year at either the pavilion or the nearby Park Pavilion in Egerton Park.

Left Shaw arrives at the pavilion for the opening of his play.

Right, top Such leading playwrights as
J.B. Priestley acclaimed the Forsyth Players'
weekly repertory performances of their work.

Right, centre and bottom The varied programme of
entertainments featured such world-class performers
as Fritz Kreisler, the leading violinist of the period.

Forsyth's crowning achievement was the British premiere at the pavilion of George Bernard Shaw's play *The Millionairess* in November 1936. Shaw himself attended, receiving an almost royal welcome at the matinee performance. Largely as a result of Forsyth's efforts, Bexhill was rapidly making a name for itself. The following year Forsyth took the play on tour with his company, visiting, among other destinations, Bath, Cambridge and Westcliff. By 1938 the Forsyth Players' performances in Bexhill were receiving good reviews in the national press.

The official opening by no means marked the end of the architectural development of the pavilion. In July 1936 new drawings were published by the Mendelsohn and Chermayeff practice that proposed further work on the initial pavilion scheme. Included in the extended designs were proposals for a cinema complex to be added to the building's eastern side, while an eight-storey hotel would join on to the building to the west, replacing the existing Metropole Hotel. On analysis, the designs make perfect sense. The long and low restaurant east wing had never satisfactorily balanced the much larger auditorium wing to the west, while its position, set back from the rest of the building to the north, had made a slightly awkward corner. Placing a cinema further east made this corner part of an enclosed square, and meant that both facilities – auditorium and cinema – would have easy access to the restaurant. Similarly, the hotel to the west would counter any criticism of the dominance of the main auditorium wing, and would continue the line of the building horizontally as the ground fell further away down the slope towards the seafront. This scheme would have had the additional benefit of protecting the seafront terrace from the effects of the weather by helping to screen the wind, which has always been a problem on the open site.

While the design drawings may not have been published until 1936, earlier sketches by Mendelsohn from 1934 suggest that this much larger concept for the entire site had been in the architect's mind all along, as part of a kind of 'wish-list' of developments that Mendelsohn hoped the council would consider for future years as and when it could afford them. The proposed scheme, had it been completed, would have been unique in Britain at the time: a complete leisure facility that made it possible for a visiting tourist, conference delegate or local resident never to have to leave the complex. Alas, the extensions to the project never materialized: by the time they were announced, the pavilion was already under scrutiny for going over budget, an ongoing issue that was to trouble it for decades to come.

Nevertheless, Bexhill had already demonstrated what was possible at the seaside, and had succeeded in its bold, modern experiment to lift the "gloom and dreariness" of the more traditional resorts that Earl De La Warr had so derided. But it fell to a delegation of foreign mayors visiting the town in 1935 to summarize what made the pavilion so exciting for the new age: "Your seaside is socialism in practice." The experiment continues to this day.

Below The Southern Railway company heavily promoted its new services throughout the 1930s. Bexhill had appeal for all kinds of visitors.

Below Although not totally accurate, this stylized poster from the 1930s highlights the pavilion's seaside location.

BEXHILL-on-SEA
Write to De La Warr Pavilion, Bexhill, for free Guide
FREQUENT ELECTRIC AND STEAM TRAINS.... CHEAP FARES BY
SOUTHERN RAILWAY

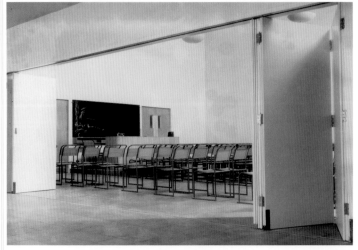

Below Until it was demolished in 1955,
the neighbouring Metropole Hotel cast an afternoon
shadow over the south terraces of the pavilion.

For three promising years after its opening in 1935, the De La Warr Pavilion was celebrated as one of the finest centres of its kind in the land. Its bold, new architecture had received the highest praise; the Forsyth Players had firmly established themselves as a leading theatre repertory company; and eminent musicians, actors and other entertainers from around the world had performed there to packed audiences. Numerous sporting, leisure and social activities had taken place, and the auditorium and restaurant had played host to thousands who danced the night away. Despite the pavilion's critics, the vision had, more or less, become a reality. But by 1939 war loomed in Europe, and the mood of enlightened optimism that had so characterized the earlier part of the decade was destroyed by Hitler's ambitions. Like many of its neighbouring southern coastal towns, Bexhill was on the front line of defence.

The summer of 1939 was particularly fine. The warm sunshine of August brought many visitors to the coast, with record numbers filling the hotels, apartments and beaches and, according to accounts in the local newspaper, creating a sell-out season for the pavilion's varied programme of all-day entertainment. By the end of the month, however, Bexhill, like the rest of the country, was facing the threat of blackout. On 3 September war was declared. Within half an hour of the announcement on the BBC by the prime minister, Neville Chamberlain, the first air-raid siren was sounded

from the pavilion's roof. During this time of crisis the pavilion came to provide the very facilities the town needed, as the defence of the realm was combined with wider war efforts to maintain the nation's morale. Yet, like many of those who frequented it during the next six years, the building did not survive the war unscathed.

While the rest of the country lived through the early 'phoney' war of the winter and early spring of 1939 and 1940 before the true force of the conflict hit home, for Britain's southern coastline the impact was immediate. The blackout meant that no night-time illuminations of any kind were allowed within 12 miles (19 km) of the south coast. With war declared, the government swiftly took further precautionary measures, temporarily closing all places of entertainment in case enemy bombers should target buildings where large assemblies of people might gather. Although the pavilion reopened two weeks later when restrictions were eased, it was clear that it had a difficult time ahead.

By October the building's first floor was requisitioned by the Ministry of Defence to house the operating arm of its southern command. Records are scant but, by 1941, three companies of the Army's 70th Battalion had their headquarters in the town. They had been brought together to undertake 'battle training' for the first time, in the Hastings and Bexhill areas, and were billeted

Right The Forsyth Players persevered with repertory until 1940, when recreational visits to the coast were banned by the government.

in local accommodation, including the convent. The loss of the use of the first floor meant that the pavilion's upstairs bar, or 'buffet', had to be found a new home, at first in the building's main foyer. It was a generally unpopular move given the reluctance, not only of the local population, to be seen drinking in public. The library and reading room, too, were closed down, the books boxed up and the furniture removed at some stage during the war. None of Chermayeff's carefully selected, powder-blue PLAN chairs was seen again after the war. The following year, 1940, the relocation of the library to a new site at the town's Green Tea Rooms caused controversy, with the £160 cost of refitting the rooms to accommodate the books criticized in the local paper as unnecessary at such a time of want.

The first days of the war also saw the largest ever mass movement of people in British history. In the first four days of September 1939, nearly 1,250,000 people were evacuated from their homes, largely in London and elsewhere in south-east England, and many fled Bexhill for refuge beyond the immediate targets of enemy bombers. In July 1940 almost half the town's school-children, 850 in all, were evacuated in a single day, taking the long train journey from Bexhill to destinations in Hertfordshire and the Home Counties, away from the increasingly real danger of bombing and invasion. Coincidentally, much of the responsibility for organizing the evacuation had fallen to Earl De La Warr

himself. As president of the Board of Education, he had been one of only six cabinet ministers who had met with Chamberlain to insist that Britain declare war on Germany if it refused to quit Poland; and he was also the man to whom responsibility for school evacuations had fallen immediately after the decision was announced.

The evacuation was to have severe consequences for the pavilion. By the start of 1941, the town council reported that it had no fewer than 1225 empty properties on its books – more than double the previous year's figure – and was owed almost £100,000 in rate arrears. With sharply declining revenues, and little immediate prospect of recovering the debts owed, the council had to find ways of reducing costs. The decision to dispense with anything non-essential to the maintenance of basic services might have been considered not only sensible but also imperative under the circumstances. However, perhaps enlightened by the effect its pavilion 'experiment' had had on the local population in previous years, the council decided to maintain 'entertainment' in some form at the De La Warr Pavilion throughout the war years, with remarkable success.

Two long weeks after war had been declared, the fear of immediate attack passed. No sooner had the government lifted its restrictions on the re-opening of entertainments halls and

Below The mayor of Bexhill and members of the council join the Army taking the salute in front of the pavilion on Empire Day, 1941.

Below Bexhill was home to three companies of the Army's 70th Battalion, which used the pavilion for drill and exercises throughout the war.

cinemas than the council's entertainments committee announced that programmes would recommence as soon as possible at the pavilion. Repertory theatre had been enjoying a sustained period of success throughout the late 1930s, and Bexhill's Forsyth Players, championed by George Bernard Shaw and J.B. Priestley, were very popular. The company swiftly staged a new production, Reginald Berkeley's *French Leave*, which played to packed audiences. As a former Royal Air Forceman, Matthew Forsyth had answered the nation's call to duty and rejoined the force at the outbreak of war, leaving the company in the hands of one of his leading players, Reginald Selleck.

By November 1939 the pavilion was filled again with visitors in search of entertainment to distract them from the gloomy news abroad. The Forsyth Players formed the highlight of the week, putting on productions on Saturdays. Variety concerts packed the hall again on Sundays (weekly now, instead of the previous twice-monthly programme). The popular Monday lectures were also reinstated, the first being given by the celebrated former journalist and broadcaster Vernon Bartlett MP, whose election to parliament on an anti-appeasement ticket in 1938 made him an ideal choice for the government to engage in producing and conveying official propaganda to the masses. Bristling with state-sponsored optimism, Bartlett confidently titled his sell-out lecture in November 1939 'The War and After'. More than 1100 people each paid 1*s.*

to attend. "Not so long ago some people of little faith and no foresight took a morbid delight in referring to the Pavilion as 'another white elephant'", stated the *Bexhill-on-Sea Observer* of the pavilion's triumphant return to form (11 November 1939, p. 2). Entertaining the masses had always been one of the pavilion's principal endeavours: in wartime it had found new vigour.

In February 1940 alone the pavilion hosted a bewildering array of entertainment. The Forsyth Players performed four separate plays, including Priestley's *Dangerous Corner* and *After the Dance* by Terence Rattigan. Every Monday and Tuesday dances were held for the mayor's fund. The Maidstone and District Sports Club held a large party, while the lecture society hosted Sir Edward Grigg, under-secretary for the Ministry of Information, who gave a packed audience first-hand news from the war. The highlight of the month was the NALGO (the local government trade union) charity ball, during which the four hundred dancing revellers were interrupted by a mock air-raid siren from the band, accompanied by searching spotlights, while hundreds of leaflets, some of which offered prizes, fluttered down from the ceiling. "Bexhill – dis iss your last chance", the leaflets read in *faux* German, "Ve haf your gasworks sunk." Such black humour was born of adversity. Local bus services had been curtailed due to the blackout, and a 20-mph night-time speed restriction had been imposed to reduce the increasing number of car accidents on the region's dark, unlit

roads. As a result, evening performances at the pavilion began an hour earlier, at 7.15 pm, to enable people to catch the last bus home at 9 pm.

But while the administration was doing its best to put on a brave show of 'business as usual', by July 1940 the threat of invasion was becoming all too real. Aware that Hitler had given the order for preparations to invade England, the government was forced to act. It imposed a curfew prohibiting any night-time access to the seafront, and banned anyone from visiting the town – or any other towns along the coast – for holidays, recreation, pleasure or casual trips. The stretch of coast between Bexhill and Eastbourne, with its flatlands and shallow sea defences, made the area an ideal landing point for invading armies. The government knew that preparations had to be made. The orders had an immediate impact, and the pavilion's traditional sources of revenue rapidly started to disappear. Unable to sustain losses indefinitely, the council was left with little option other than to cut back. First to go was the pavilion's popular programme of repertory theatre. The Forsyth Players made their final appearance on the pavilion stage during the same week that the new orders were brought in, with a typically insouciant production of Fred Jackson's comedy *The Naughty Wife*. Undeterred, the players' director, Reginald Selleck, headed down the coast with his company to Hastings, where repertory continued at the town's White Rock Pavilion.

Although repertory had closed, the council insisted that the pavilion would remain open for entertainment, with the musical trio still playing three times daily in the café on the ground floor. But the café's demise, too, soon followed that of the theatre. Only the year before, catering at the pavilion café had notched up record profits, £1721 in the year to March 1940, compared with just £520 the previous year, making a healthy contribution to the building's overall operating costs. By July 1940, however, profits had turned rapidly to losses, which were rising to almost £10 per week. Already running on a skeleton staff, the restaurant was closed in August.

Left While dances continued during wartime, the demand for military personnel meant that other performances soon began to be curtailed.

Above Lectures continued during the war. There were even well-attended demonstrations of cooking with wartime rations.

Below In September 1940 sixteen bombs fell on Bexhill in one day alone, as this cutting from the *Bexhill-on-Sea Observer* reports. The pavilion itself was not spared.

Two men from the café were retained after the restaurant's closure, one to serve as night watchman, the other to act as air-raid attendant, starting up the whining siren on the pavilion's roof at any hint of an impending bombing raid. Although warnings had occurred since the outbreak of war, no bombs had so far landed anywhere near Bexhill. However, the Luftwaffe's focus on bombing airfields to win supremacy in the skies – crucial for any invasion plans – was suddenly switched in September 1940 to bombing towns and cities in an attempt to break the nation's resolve. Bexhill was right in the firing line.

Many people believed that the bombing had already made its mark on the town in May that year, when the Metropole Hotel, the Edwardian towers of which had hemmed the neighbouring pavilion into its tightly measured site, caught fire in a spectacular blaze. In fact, the fire, which damaged much of the building, was caused not by any incendiary device but instead started in one of the top-floor bedrooms. In September, however, the bombing began in earnest and, just after 8 am on the morning of 30 September, sixteen bombs fell on the town. The pavilion was itself hit by a massive bomb that fell through the auditorium roof, exploded inside and caused substantial damage to the western end wall as well as to the stage, lighting equipment and backstage areas. The air-raid attendant described how, as the dust settled, he peered through the gaping holes in the wall and saw that the Metropole, already closed as a result of the fire, lay in ruins. If anything, the pavilion had had a lucky escape. Throughout the Battle of Britain and the subsequent Blitz, air raids were an almost daily occurrence in the town, tailing off only in May 1941 when Hitler's attention was diverted to the Eastern Front. The lull lasted until 1942, which became known as the 'tip-and-run' year. A plane, or several planes, would suddenly swoop in from the sea, release some bombs indiscriminately, rake the town with machine-gun fire and then dash out again. The pavilion, with its bright, white walls glimmering in the sun, was also a highly visible landmark for bombers heading back to northern France, a final destination for raids should they have any bombs left in their cargo. In addition, Bexhill was in the direct flight path of 'Bomb Alley' (stretching from the south coast of England up to London) during the brief and

FIVE PEOPLE RESCUED FROM WRECKED HOUSE

HEROIC TEAM WORK

BOMBS BLAST WINDOWS AND KILL HORSES

After a bomb fell outside a cinema, this picture was produced.

THE MAYOR'S RELIEF FUND

IMMEDIATE HELP FOR AIR RAID VICTIMS

CENTRAL WELFARE FUND

DE LA WARR PAVILION

WEDNESDAY, APRIL 15th, at 7.30 p.m.

CONCERT

Admission 2/-, 1/- and 6d. H.M. Navy, Army and R.A.F. Free

Doors Open 7.0 p.m.

SATURDAY, APRIL 18th, 7.30 - 11.45 p.m.

DANCE

Jack Shaw and his Orchestra

Admission (including Refreshments) 2/6

(H.M. Navy, Army and R.A.F. 1/6)

BEXHILL ROTARY CLUB

Above To lift spirits, the Rotary Club started organizing dances in aid of servicemen's welfare.

Bottom, left Comedian Spike Milligan (second from right) plays jazz trumpet in the wartime gunners' band.

Bottom, right Dancing became the single most popular form of wartime relaxation, and the pavilion's Easter dances were no exception.

Below, top and bottom On some evenings the auditorium was transformed into a hall for boxing tournaments.

unsuccessful attempt by Hitler to beat Britain into submission with volleys of flying bombs aimed at the capital city. In 1944 no fewer than 480 flying bombs were tracked passing over the town during one period of twenty-four hours, and, although some were to fall in Bexhill during the course of that year, only one soldier lost his life as a result.

There were initial fears that the bomb damage had knocked the entertainments hall out of action for the duration of the war. Recognizing that hibernation in the winter months was not good for public morale, the Rotary Club stepped in, persuading the council and the townspeople that the pavilion might once again be reopened, for social functions at least. Mayor Cuthbert took up the idea, reversing an earlier council decision to close the building for the foreseeable future, and granted the Rotary Club use of the building to run events in aid of various armed forces or prisoner of war funds.

For Christmas 1940 the Rotary Club organized its first dance. The bomb-damaged stage was decorated with a large Union Jack, while a five-piece military jazz band played before the large Wadsworth mural, specially removed from the wall of the restaurant to form a decorative backdrop to proceedings. What lights had not been destroyed in the attack were played on the dance floor, where revellers heard Stanley Courtenay, the Rotary president and master of ceremonies for the evening, thank the council for its generosity. "The feeling I have," he said, "is that, now the ice has been broken and this building has been made available, it has opened up an entirely new vista in the life of the town, especially while our guests [the visiting troops] are with us." More dances followed on New Year's Eve, and during subsequent years, the pavilion extended its role as morale-booster. In March 1941 the Rotary Club inaugurated a programme of boxing tournaments that continued throughout the war and proved highly popular with the troops and local residents. Contestants were drawn from the civilian population and service boxing ranks. Concerts by military bands replaced the restaurant trio. Spike Milligan, then a young artillery gunner, became a familiar face, playing jazz

Below From 1941 the Women's Voluntary Service
ran the British Restaurant in the pavilion's cafeteria,
serving wholesome meals at 9*d*. a time.

trumpet with the gunners' band from nearby Hastings Road. Milligan was to 'celebrate' his stationing in Bexhill in later years in such Goons sketches as 'The Dreaded Batter-Pudding Hurler of Bexhill-on-Sea' and in his book *Adolf Hitler: My Part in his Downfall* (1971), his own zany take on the war.

In August 1941 the Women's Voluntary Service, under the leadership of the mayor's wife, reopened the pavilion's café as the British Restaurant, transferring from the nearby Park Pavilion to its new, larger home. In one year alone, a team of fourteen women served up 34,500 meals, providing healthy, communal eating for both servicemen and locals, all for just 9*d*. a meal.

The reason for the disappearance of the pavilion's familiar 'roundels' is still the subject of speculation. These circular name-plates had graced the building from its opening but, according to photographic records, they disappeared at some point during the war. One explanation is that they were removed in response to the call to the nation, in August 1941, for any kind of available scrap metal to be donated to the war effort. The campaign saw the town collect a remarkable 57 tonnes of scrap in just two weeks, putting surplus pots, pans, balustrades and decorations into a huge pile in Devonshire Road, ready to be carted away. Some maintain that the south wall roundel would not have survived the bomb attack on the pavilion and the adjacent Metropole Hotel. Others argue that the council removed the signs in order to avoid the building, designed by a German Jew and named after an English cabinet minister, being targeted by bombers. Whatever the reason for the roundels' disappearance, they were replaced with replicas only in the 1990s, after fundraising appeals by the Pavilion Trust.

However much the town sought to steel itself against the ravages of wartime, the pavilion building was in a sorry state. With the D-Day landings of 1944, the threat of full-scale bombings on British soil finally diminished. Bexhill, like the rest of the nation, could start to think about rebuilding. To determine just how badly the pavilion had been damaged, the council commissioned a detailed report from Hannes Schreiner, Mendelsohn's assistant architect, who had worked on the original drawings for the building and had remained in Britain throughout the war. Schreiner's investigations in fact went further than an assessment of structural damage. Eager that the pavilion should continue with its popular new wartime entertainments, particularly dancing, the council asked Schreiner to suggest improvements to the building, and highlight any additions that could be made.

Although none of Schreiner's proposals was actually implemented, other than essential repairs to the bomb-damaged areas, his *Report on War Damage and Dilapidations and Suggestions for Improvements and Additions for the Entertainments Committee of the Borough of Bexhill* of September 1944 included ideas that formed the basis of much of the work on the pavilion that

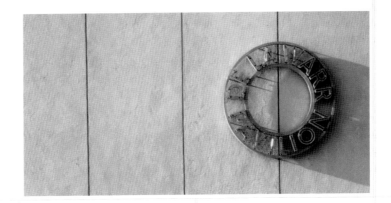

successive council administrations commissioned in later years. In its genesis, Mendelsohn had conceived a simple scheme, the design of which was intended to enable society to move towards an enlightened age of leisure pursuit. Without doubt, the war dealt a blow to such aspirations, and the current council's aims were to make the pavilion suitable for 'party functions', dances and popular entertainment.

Despite the evident cracking of rendered finishes in many areas of the building, Schreiner concluded that the 1940 bombing had not had the great structural impact that had first been feared. The building's west wall would have to be demolished so that the horizontal beams and stanchions could once more be tied in, but little other structural work was needed. The back wall to the stage needed rebuilding, a staircase needed replacing and the dressing rooms, destroyed by the impact of the blast, would have to be reinstated. The report also considered in detail a wide variety of other improvements, recommending the replacement of broken aluminium door handles with steel ones, better extraction and ventilation in the kitchen area to reduce condensation, and new arrangements for the auditorium's orchestra pit and seating in order to allow the floor to be cleared more efficiently for dances and other functions. Schreiner's principal suggestions were for a number of additions to the building's overall scheme, including two new bar areas, a soda fountain and a major new dance hall, to be built adjoining the pavilion's north wall, at the eastern corner. One bar was to be positioned on the south terrace, leading off from the auditorium and facing out to sea. It was suggested that this addition would "allow for a future connection between the Pavilion and a possible hotel to the West of the site". Another bar was envisaged under the building's main entrance, created by excavating beneath the building, with direct access from either the auditorium foyer or the south terrace.

Schreiner also recognized that times had changed and that the "present arrangement of making the Theatre use a dual purpose will not be satisfactory in the future as there will be a great demand for dances and it will be a great asset to the Town to be able to run dances every night". To this end, he proposed that the new dance hall be constructed at first-floor level, connecting to a reconfigured lounge made up of the former sun lounge and part of the original reading room and library. This, in turn, would be served by a restored bar area on the first floor, while the entrance to the hall would be via a new foyer that would lead straight out on to the Marine Parade, the whole dance hall forming a bridge under which vehicles could gain access to the car park. But, at an estimated cost of £53,000 for the dance hall extension alone, Schreiner's proposals were to prove too expensive for a council only just recovering from war. The impact of the proposals was profound, however: they confirmed the opinion that the pavilion in its original form was no longer entirely suitable for the new uses for which it was now required. Although commissioned in the spirit of progress, the report was to herald a prolonged period of architectural decline.

chapter 7   the pavilion in decline

"We may allow ourselves a brief period of rejoicing", announced Winston Churchill, the British prime minister, at the end of the war in Europe in May 1945. And rejoice the British certainly did, flocking to the palaces of entertainment as their loved ones returned from combat. The De La Warr Pavilion, its bomb damage now patched up, was ready for the challenge.

Although the building was still in poor repair, the council's first step was to reinstate the pavilion's popular programme of repertory theatre. It appointed the Reunion Players, a new troupe led by Pat Nye and Campbell Singer comprising men and women with stage experience who had recently been released from military service. They were an instant hit. In just ten weeks of repertory, more than 28,000 theatregoers saw the players' productions of *School for Scandal*, *Macbeth*, *Henry V* and *Rebecca*.

In 1947 a pattern was established for the entertainments programme that was to last until 1960. A new summer show would be staged every year, with repertory theatre performing for the rest of the year. Musical concerts would still be put on in the auditorium when acts could be arranged. Throughout 1946 and 1947 the concerts played to capacity audiences, with the world-famous piano duo Rawicz and Landauer and the celebrated Austrian tenor Richard Tauber proving especially popular. With the band crammed on to the pavilion's stage, Felix Mendelssohn and

his Hawaiian Serenaders were equally well received, their performance evoking life on exotic isles far removed from the austerity of rationing, imitation coffee and demob clothing.

While the pavilion was enjoying success front of house, backstage it was a different matter. The dressing rooms to the north of the west end had been destroyed in the war, while those to the south were also damaged. Hannes Schreiner's report of 1944 had also identified that a beam tying one of the main stanchions to the west wall had been seriously damaged, and had advised the replacement of all the end structural members and reconstruction of the dressing rooms, the plenum chamber and the main west wall itself. Cracks had appeared in the auditorium's exterior, too, and the report highlighted a number of other areas where the building was showing signs of stress.

The estimate for making good the wartime dilapidations came to £7245, while a further £8048 was estimated for reinstatement works. Although the report went into considerable detail, by no means does it appear that all the work proposed was carried out. Cork tiles were not replaced, neither was the building's neon sign, nor the duckboards in the roof gutters; the north elevation was not cleaned as suggested; the canopy, balustrade and supporting wall were not renewed; and the crack that had emerged in the main foyer's terrazzo flooring was not repaired. Nevertheless, some essential repairs to the pavilion were carried out, and in June 1948 a payment of £8250 was made for the work that had been completed to date. The cost of work to be done in connection with the theatre under the direction of the then consultant architect was estimated at a further £8500.

That same year the council decided a change was needed to its entertainments programming, and it replaced the Reunion Players with a new repertory company called the Century Players. However, the switch was unpopular and the negative publicity that resulted had an impact on audiences, which started to tail off dramatically. As a result, in 1950 the Century Players were themselves replaced with the Penguin Players, a company run by Richard Burnett that had been successful with its plays at the recently refurbished Egerton Park Theatre nearby. The decision this time proved much more popular. Within a brief period, the players were taken on as repertory company contracted to the council, and they continued to play at both the pavilion and Egerton Park for the next twenty-five years.

The work that the Penguin Players put into their productions was hard and relentless. While one show was being performed, up to three or four more were being rehearsed, planned, designed or marketed. The following week's sets had to be painted, props hunted down in local antique shops, and scenery adapted from earlier productions. With funding tight, the task of staging a new play every week taxed even the most inventive of producers. Financial difficulties were by no means the sole preserve of the repertory company, however. Never fully restored after the war, the entire auditorium and backstage area constantly seemed to require new innovations to keep it open. Former stage director Leslie Steen, who had joined the pavilion as chief engineer two months before it opened in 1935, recalled in the 1970s:

The worst piece of design was the system for removing the auditorium seats for dances. The intention was that the seats should be stacked under the raised side aisles. But the doors provided were not high enough and only a few rows of seats could be accommodated. I produced a sort of Heath Robinson contraption which everyone thought was very funny at the time. We just put the seats on a see-saw, and tipped them down a chute under the stage: looked ridiculous but worked like a charm.

(*Bexhill-on-Sea Observer*, 30 May 1970)

The pavilion stumbled on with another of Steen's inventions for almost thirty-five years: an array of stage lights made out of disused oil drums, painted inside, with a large mirror fitted behind each light. This innovative design worked perfectly. The lights were only superseded – at considerably greater cost – when the mirrors became impossible to replace.

28491. BEXHILL - ON - SEA THE DE LA WARR PAVILION. · JUDGES LTD

Left For a time during the 1950s the pavilion's smooth, cream exterior became smothered in creeping ivy.

Above and opposite For a decade from 1951, the pavilion hosted a hugely popular summer show, *Starlight Rendevous*. Staged daily, it featured top comedians, jugglers, singers and ventriloquists, among other performers.

Perhaps unsurprisingly, the pavilion theatre also proved a successful training ground for a number of young hopefuls eager to get on the first rung of the performing ladder. Andrew Sachs, later familiar to TV audiences for his role as Manuel in the comedy series *Fawlty Towers*, served a spell as assistant stage manager at the pavilion in the 1950s before going on to become an actor.

For performers, the post-war years were a time of opportunity. With the end of petrol rationing in 1950, car ownership rocketed, and suburbanites flocked to the seaside for day trips and short stays in the hotels and bed-and-breakfast establishments that sprang up to cater for the new trade. Providing day-long programmes of entertainment, the pavilion's summer shows were a great success. In 1951 the pavilion first staged Edward Kent's *Starlight Rendezvous*, a summer show that enjoyed a long run throughout the following decade. In its first year, headlined by the comedian Freddie Frinton, the show attracted audiences totalling almost 62,000 people. Frinton returned for three further seasons in subsequent years. Interspersed between summer shows and repertory theatre were classical concerts, the highlight of which was a visit by Sir Thomas Beecham with the Royal Philharmonic Orchestra in January 1949. In 1960 the newly appointed entertainments and publicity manager, Rupert Lockwood, initiated a successful series of annual music festivals in which Manchester's Hallé Orchestra, under conductor Sir John Barbirolli, played a leading part.

Even though audience numbers in the 1940s and 1950s were buoyant, and the acts clearly highly popular, the pavilion was still losing money. Considerable deficits had built up during the war, while any proceeds from the popular dances at the time had been donated largely to the war effort or troops' funds. With rationing still in place, and the nation rebuilding its shattered homes, few families had much money to spend, which meant that the pavilion was forced to keep entrance prices at low rates. Even the more successful ventures made little mark on revenues.

The cost of essential repairs to the war damage had drained valuable resources from the council's coffers. Little was left over for equally essential running repairs, many of which were the result of past neglect. Most visible of these problems were the pavilion's steel window frames, originally selected on the grounds of economy over the preferred corrosion-proof bronze, but now rusting badly and cracking the glazing in places. Yet the council could barely afford the new paint. And while the weather and the wear and tear caused by thousands of visitors a week took their toll, the pavilion's team was also struggling with the constant need to adapt the building to new demands for dances and increased bar and catering facilities, few of which were operating efficiently.

From 1951 to 1961, the average annual bill for repairs to the pavilion ran to £3560, a heavy cost made more difficult to reduce

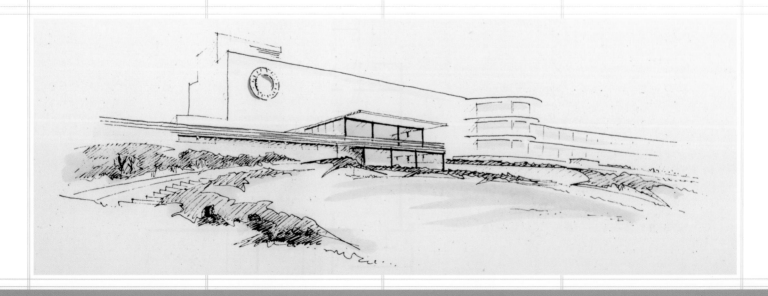

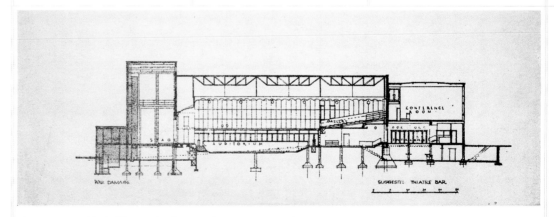

GENERAL SUMMARY OF ALL ESTIMATED COSTS.

WAR DAMAGE	..	£8,048
DILAPIDATIONS	..	£7,245
REMOVAL OF AIR RAID PRECAUTIONS	..	£150
		£15,443

SUGGESTED IMPROVEMENTS and ADDITIONS.

(a) Door handles ..	..	£552
(b) Window plaques ..		£930
	Alternatively	£277
(c) New "IN" and "OUT" Signs to Car Park ..	}	£100
(d) False ceilings and ventilation to Kitchens and Services	}	£181
(e) Booking Office ..	..	£58
(f) Band platform and hood ..		£54
(g) Terrazzo pavings	..	£280
(h) Amplification System	..	£150
(j) Stage	..	£200
(k) Alteration to existing foot lights ..		£150
(l) Alteration to house openings		£68
(m) Boxing ring lighting	..	£30
(n) Seating in Auditorium	..	£565
(o) Soda Fountain ..	..	£300
(p) Licensed bar accommodation and Green Room ..	}	£16,000
(q) Theatre refreshment bar	..	£7,000
(r) Dance Hall ..	..	£53,000

by the fact that no part of the building could be closed down (except for one day in the year, Christmas Day). On one occasion, when painters began to chip away rust from the external metalwork, the noise could be heard throughout the building. The patrons complained, and the entire job had be called off. When one part of the building was redecorated, any equipment displaced by the work had to be stored elsewhere. The pavilion had been built with no spare capacity.

By 1955 the council could wait no longer, and major modification plans were drawn up by its architects, based loosely on Hannes Schreiner's original proposals of 1944. Lack of funds, however, meant that the new proposals focused only on how the pavilion could be rearranged internally, rather than creating the generous additional space for which Schreiner had already predicted demand ten years earlier. Moreover, once the work on modifying the pavilion's interior was started, it set in motion a process of near-constant minor modifications to the building's configurations, none of which dealt satisfactorily with the problems.

For example, after the war the council recognized the need for a medium-sized dance hall, for informal functions and smaller musical events. Its solution was to create a new function room on the east wing's first floor. The sun parlour was enclosed, the reading room extended to the west, and a new bar installed in the dance hall. The existing bar was reduced in size and relocated to what had formerly been the still room next door.

The reconfiguration meant that two of the building's original functions had now been lost: the reading room and library, championed by Earl De La Warr for the literary enlightenment of his townsfolk; and the external sun parlour, to promote the health and well-being of the Bexhill residents. The building's new decor was anthema from a Modernist perspective. The council had already dismantled what was left of the luxurious wood-veneered bookcases and transferred them to the public library. The new

Above A section of the building, used to illustrate Schreiner's report, reveals war-damaged areas and proposals for a sunken bar area beneath the auditorium foyer.

dance hall bar was decorated in *faux* brick and stone, as part of a general scheme to replace the original simple, clean lines and colours of the building's interior with what was thought to be a more intimate, contemporary decor.

The changes met with the approval of the local hoteliers association, since the new function room would, it said, "be of great value in propagating visits by conference delegates". Conference bookings were certainly needed: by the mid-1950s the pavilion's summer audience numbers were falling rapidly. The advent of the first package holidays to Spain's Costa del Sol in 1954 sparked an almost immediate decline in the popularity of the traditional British seaside holiday, and tourists flocked there in their thousands. For the south of England's coastal resorts, the new trend was a disaster. Between 1954 and 1961 nearly all of Bexhill's main hotels closed. The Marine Mansions was demolished in 1954 and the bomb-damaged Metropole the following year; the Devonshire closed in 1957 and the Sackville in 1960. The Riposo was pulled down in 1961 to make way for what was the town's only growth industry at the time, retirement flats.

Other forces were at play, too. Although many schools had returned to Bexhill after the war, their number declined steadily over the following years. Most of the schools were boarding, catering largely for children of the overseas armed forces and of

the colonial administration. But the steady break-up of the British Empire and, in particular, the granting of independence to India in 1947 hastened their demise. Schools and tourism had been the lynchpins of Bexhill's former prosperity, yet both were now declining. Far from being a tourist destination, the town was becoming more like a retirement village. Therefore, by the time the council had finally undertaken the first of many alterations to keep the building in tune with changes in demand, much of the pavilion's audience had moved on. The pavilion was burdened by the capital costs of the extensions and also facing sharply falling attendances; far from improving the pavilion's finances, the refurbishments seemed only to hasten the decline.

By 1960 it was clear that the pavilion needed to change once again in order to adjust to the downturn in visitor numbers. Although Rupert Lockwood, the new entertainments and publicity manager, had experience and contacts from the conference trade, the loss of the town's hotels made it clear this was not a viable business for the pavilion to pursue. Even though the pavilion could provide conference facilities, there were no longer enough hotels in the town to accommodate the delegates satisfactorily. As a result, with his team, Lockwood put forward a number of proposals for altering the building to make it appeal more to local users, with better facilities for social activities on a smaller scale, and the provision of shelter for music patrons on the terrace. Lockwood's

proposal was for the ground-floor restaurant to be extended out on to the south terrace, to enable dinner-and-dances to take place, while also providing for bigger kitchens to cope with the extra demand for food. Although the scheme never progressed, by early 1962 the council was coming under increasing criticism for doing nothing, and could not fail to acknowledge that, after twenty-six years of almost constant service, the building was beginning to look shabby. There was an almost constant battle against the rusting windows; dirt had not been removed from the building's exterior and had now worked its way into the Cullamix render, causing it to craze and the dirt become ingrained; and tiles on the pillars were cracked. And, despite the 1955 alterations, the building was still not operating efficiently. A further report was commissioned.

The council had received an over-ambitious document from Schreiner's London office in 1944; its own architects had perhaps not gone far enough with their proposals a decade later; now, in 1962, it sought to find a sound, long-term solution to the pavilion's problems. The firm of architects selected, Henry Ward & Partners, was based in nearby Hastings and had itself worked on several modern buildings on the coast. The proposals in Ward's report, almost all of which were subsequently acted on, took the building yet further away from its original design intentions. For example, the increase in bar trade had long caused all sorts of storage problems with crates and empty bottles. Ward's solution was to reduce the size of the kitchens and build a storeroom. The problem of moving supplies around the building, particularly up and down the stairs, was solved by Ward's proposal to install a goods' lift next to the store, with another serving the new bar in the function room upstairs. The central bar serving all three rooms upstairs had caused problems, with noise from functions interrupting meetings in the lecture room, and vice versa. Ward proposed building a new, separate bar out into the upstairs lounge served by three new rooms carved out of the former lecture theatre: a storeroom, a room for stacked chairs, and the lift housing. The location of the new rooms, however, meant that access to the lecture room's ceiling-level windows was blocked. As a result, a false ceiling was installed, blotting out the natural light altogether. Bigger bars

required more toilets, so proposals for these were included, taking out another section of the restaurant and the function room upstairs. The relocation of the manager's office, and the need for the kitchens themselves to be larger to serve the three bars and function rooms, reduced the size of the restaurant, making it appear much narrower than before. Consequently, the dance floor at the end of the restaurant was dispensed with, and the room was divided into a table-service restaurant at one end and a self-service cafeteria at the other.

An alternative scheme for improvements was put forward later that same year by Maxwell Fry, one of the contestants for the building's original design. Fry proposed enlarging the east wing by pushing the north wall out into the car park by 3 m (10 ft) in order to house offices and new kitchens, but keeping the restaurant intact. The council opted for Ward's scheme and, by the middle of 1963, the scheme of 'improvements' was largely complete. Yet this was not the end of the story. In November of that year, the pavilion posted near-record deficits, as the cost of the alterations was met and revenue lost while they were being undertaken. Any new money-making idea was considered: a tenpin bowling alley was proposed for the roof, for example, but the idea was swiftly dropped when structural engineers reported that the roof would need to be strengthened. A colour movie was commissioned, a copy of which still survives in the Bexhill Museum, to play at cinemas in an unsuccessful bid to attract visitors to the town. Even Queen Elizabeth II was enlisted to rally support, with her visit to the pavilion in 1966 drawing large crowds.

Still the pavilion struggled to find a solution to its problems. The town's increasingly elderly population was adding further pressures. Even though a second handrail had been installed in 1956, older residents were finding the stairs difficult to master, thus reducing still further the clientele for any of the upstairs facilities. Evening performances were suffering, too, particularly in winter, with fewer residents willing to venture out after dark to an austere and sometimes draughty pavilion. In 1967 yet more work was undertaken to try to make the pavilion feel more welcoming and entice the locals out to events. The upstairs function room was

Below Although the 1960s conversion of the reading room allowed the space to be used for dances, it gave the room the look of an upturned boat.

Below Pot plants and trailing ivy bedecked every corner of the building, including the famous staircase.

Opposite A visit to the pavilion by Queen Elizabeth in 1966 drew large crowds, but audiences in general were dwindling.

redesigned in a different style, with sloping tongue-and-grooved walls that curved to meet the suspended ceiling, painted brown, resembling the upturned hull of a boat. Mendelsohn's slender central columns were clad in timber. The floor was covered with brown carpet, with a central alleyway of parquet for dancing. To separate the function room from the lounge bar, the glazed dividing wall was boarded over and covered with heavily patterned wallpaper. The room was renamed the Elizabeth room, after the visit the previous year by the monarch. The lounge bar, too, was redecorated in a similar vein: a richly patterned carpet covered the floor; the familiar bulbous lamps were replaced with inexpensive contemporary lights; frilly curtains softened the edges. The former lecture theatre, now greatly reduced in size, was renamed the Edinburgh room, carpeted, wallpapered in swirling anaglypta and filled with Formica-topped tables for meetings and other functions. It relied completely on electric light. Nowhere was spared this decorative overhaul. Rubber plants filled every corner. The building's great spiral staircase was bedecked with ivy and begonias, which cascaded down its curves. The foyer was filled with plants, vending machines and advertising hoardings for local shops and services. But the pavilion was out of step with the times. The young in 1960s Britain liked to eat in modern, plastic Wimpy Bars and garish Golden Egg restaurants; they went to nightclubs and contemporary bars, the cinema and pop concerts. In 1969 the repertory theatre posted an annual loss of £29,716, almost

£600 per week, at a time when a household's average weekly grocery bill was £3.

Not all of the pavilion alterations were driven by the need to generate revenue. In the wake of the Isle of Man Summerlands disaster of 1973, in which a fire in a poorly equipped leisure centre claimed fifty-one lives and injured many more, new legislation required immediate upgrading of fire exits and precautions in all public buildings. The pavilion installed new fire screens and doors to the main entrances and upstairs lobbies but, unable to meet the cost of new fire escapes, it had little option but to close the building's roof to visitors.

The pressing need for a lift was eventually tackled in 1971, yet the initial proposal caused an uproar. The council had been unable to find any detailed structural plans for the building and was apprehensive about cutting through floors for a lift shaft in case the work disturbed any steel girders. Jack Seabrook, a former council planning officer and later a key member of the Pavilion Trust, recalls the desperate search: "I remember they even lifted the commemorative plaque at the foot of the stairs because they felt sure the plans would be buried in the casket underneath. But they weren't!" (letter to Alastair Fairley, 14 March 2003, De La Warr Pavilion Archive). L.S. Jay, the county planning officer, wrote to Serge Chermayeff, who was living in Wellfleet, Massachusetts, to

Pages 128–29 In the 1960s Bexhill made a promotional film in order to compete with the new fashion for package holidays abroad. The pavilion featured strongly since it remained the town's principal tourist attraction, as these stills from the film demonstrate.

Below, left In the 1970s the bandstand was replaced with a large, brick-built version dominating the view from the terrace.

Below, right The new bandstand replaced the one built after the war from timber and canopies salvaged from the demolished Metropole Hotel.

ask if he had any plans or an idea of their whereabouts. Doing his best to appease the architect by informing him that the building had by then been identified as one of architectural and historical interest, Jay went on to explain that the council proposed installing a lift "enclosed by a cylindrical shaft faced with wood and set concentrically within the main spiral staircase on the south or sea side of the building" (letter to Serge Chermayeff, 24 August 1971, Erich and Louise Mendelsohn Papers). Chermayeff was incensed. Not only could he not help with any plans (his own had been destroyed in a bombing raid on his London offices during the war), his reply was unequivocal: "The Bexhill proposal is, of course, an installation which is guaranteed to destroy the central feature of the Pavilion from the architectural historic point of view." But he did not leave it there. He wrote to the secretary of the RIBA, requesting that the institute take action to "protect the De La Warr Pavilion from the Bexhill fathers", and wrote also to Mendelsohn's widow, Louise, in California, telling her that he had "unhappy memories of [the] Bexhill fathers after Buck De La Warr left!!" (letter to Louise Mendelsohn, 3 September 1971, Erich and Louise Mendelsohn Papers). Perhaps in order to avoid aggravating the ire of both Chermayeff and the RIBA, the council eventually found an alternative location, and installed a new lift, clad in timber boarding, in the auditorium foyer, while both the foyer and the main entrance hall were redecorated after the construction work with heavy gold-flock wallpaper.

During the 1970s, it seemed that no year went past without the council needing to undertake some form of alteration to the pavilion. In 1973 a ramp was installed to allow disabled visitors access to the building. The same year a part of the car park was screened off by a wall to provide a beer store for the kitchens, while the closing-off of the roof led the council to move the manager's offices upstairs to the top floor, which now became out of bounds to the public. In 1975 the cafeteria was renovated again, this time with hard, fixed plastic seating installed for the self-service café, with a screen erected to divide it from the waiter-service restaurant at the other end. The overall effect, as one councillor later pointed out, "was to make the Pavilion's catering facilities look more like a motorway caff". A tropical fish tank was fitted into the wall of the lobby leading to the north staircase, and a stone sculpture to commemorate the Queen's silver jubilee in 1977 was installed in a recess between the building's front doors and the fire screens leading into the main lobby. The council and the pavilion management seemed to have given up on the idea that the building was anything other than a social club for local residents, and were happy to decorate it as such. In 1977 four designs were put forward to replace the pavilion's rotting bandstand, which had itself been patched together from salvaged items from the demolished Metropole Hotel. A row of screens had already been erected to protect audiences on the terrace from the wind. To this, in 1978, was added a new bandstand, built at a

WEST LAWN FROM DE LA WARR PAVILION, BEXHILL-ON-SEA.

Below Upstairs, the warm and 'homely'
bar decor made it appear more like
a traditional pub.

Below Hard plastic seating
gave the cafeteria the feel of
a transport café.

cost of £9000, to entertain summer visitors. Other work was more mundane, though no less essential. The building's rusting steel window frames were replaced throughout the 1970s, but with timber rather than steel. In 1972 the roof of the east wing was replaced. Six years later the leaking roof of the auditorium also had to be replaced. The cost of maintaining the building was becoming a greater burden for the council.

The impact on the building's social functions was all too clear. In August 1974 the Congress Theatre in Eastbourne was still playing to full houses, with summer shows featuring the popular television star Ronnie Corbett and the singer Kenneth McKellar. Eurovision Song Contest entrant Clodagh Rodgers and entertainer Max Bygraves made Sunday appearances. Top-price tickets cost £1.35. The De La Warr Pavilion, by contrast, headlined with a Russian balalaika troupe, two plays from the Penguin Players, 'Uncle George' providing children's entertainment on Tuesdays, Thursdays and Saturdays, and 'old-tyme' dancing, with Scottish country dancing on Saturdays. The summer season's highlight was a two-day light music festival in September with the BBC Concert Orchestra. With the exception of those for the BBC Orchestra, tickets rarely cost more than 75 pence.

The Penguin Players, Bexhill's repertory company, had kept going for twenty-five years, but by 1975 their days were spent. Repertory

closed at the pavilion that year, never to return, the programme being replaced with whatever one-off presentations could be staged for the local audience. With the closure of repertory, the original purpose of the pavilion was all but forgotten. The reading room and lecture hall had been turned into a gathering place for people to shelter from the wind while having a drink. With the exception of the auditorium, almost all of the building's original rooms had been changed beyond all recognition, while the 1930s minimal approach to decoration had been transformed into a bewildering mixture of flock wallpaper, frilled curtains and house plants. The pavilion's once-famous programme of entertainment had been replaced by a routine roster of bingo, social clubs, Christmas pantomime and occasional appearances by former TV celebrities. Earl De La Warr's vision of an enlightened palace of leisure had not just been lost – it had been completely smothered.

chapter 8　　　a new dawn for the pavilion

By the mid-1970s, with its repertory company gone, the interior changed beyond all recognition, and the exterior constantly suffering the effects of wind and salt, the De La Warr Pavilion seemed doomed. Britain was in the grip of recession, and operating losses at the pavilion continued to mount. The battle between those who argued for the pavilion's upkeep and those who maintained that the town could not afford such a luxury continued to dog its Bexhill Council landlords, who had worked hard to keep the building open, patched-up and operational.

The 1980s, however, heralded a new dawn for the pavilion: one of repair, refurbishment and restoration. It was the same combination of local council, committed Bexhill citizens and well-connected lovers of the arts and architecture that first brought the building into being that was also to come to its rescue. But the process was sometimes tortuous, and there were many setbacks. At first, the signs were not good. The reorganization of local government in 1974 saw Bexhill Council subsumed into a much larger district, Rother, that brought together the administration of the town with the surrounding rural community, the ratepayers of which had even less desire than the townspeople to pay for the upkeep of a building they rarely used. Stifled by public opinion, throughout the late 1970s and early 1980s the council was able to carry out only ongoing maintenance to the pavilion's fabric. Inside, the building was rotting away.

The lack of any strategic maintenance plan for the building had led to a series of unsympathetic alterations in a hotchpotch of styles. The building's original beauty had been all but obscured by work carried out in response to sporadic operational difficulties rather than as part of a planned programme of repair. Together with spiralling operating costs, these problems were forcing the council to increase its levels of subsidy to services such as catering, civic and private functions, light entertainment, amateur theatre and music, simply to keep the building open. Run almost as a village hall with an adjoining seaside theatre, the pavilion was regarded by many as a costly, low-value-for-money liability on ratepayers. Reversing its fortunes was not going to be easy.

The first real steps came in 1983, when a number of new councillors were elected to Rother. Their attitude to the building took a new approach. They argued that, far from being a liability, the pavilion was an asset to the town, an opportunity to regenerate the area and attract visitors. They had a job on their hands. Not only were these ideas not new (they reflected Earl De La Warr's arguments when the building was first proposed), but conservation was not even on the agenda when the pavilion's maintenance issues were debated at the town hall at the time. In 1985 things came to a head over a seemingly minor issue, to the town hall, at least: that of replacing the building's front doors. The heavy glass doors were proving difficult for many of the town's elderly residents to open, and proposals were put forward for their replacement. But there was one councillor who had recently been elected to the council's recreation and tourism committee to whom the idea was anathema, not because of the cost of £14,000 for the proposed works, but on conservation grounds. Her name was Jill Theis. The building, she argued, must be protected and restored, not vandalized and altered.

Rallying allies among the council's new blood, Councillor Theis formed a small lobby group aimed at preventing the authority from undertaking further insensitive alterations to what the group recognized was a building of major significance. But the group's members knew they could not succeed alone. That same year, 1985, the councillors invited two journalists from the architectural press to visit Bexhill, ostensibly to cover the pavilion's golden jubilee celebrations. Shortly afterwards, a key article by Jonathan Glancey and David Hamilton Eddy appeared in the *RIBA Journal*, highlighting the building's international significance while bemoaning its sorry state. Architects worldwide were alerted. Contrasting the building of the present day with its original splendour, the article held no punches: "Here is a princess in rags", it declared (vol. 92, September 1985, p. 34). The description stuck. Others rallied swiftly to the cause. The British Steel Industry designated the building as a structural steel classic, while the Royal Academy's exhibition that year on the work of Richard Rogers, Norman Foster and James Stirling highlighted the pavilion as a landmark in the development of modern architecture.

The councillors knew that, while helpful, awards and publicity alone would not be sufficient to stop the building literally rotting away. Backed by David Powell, the chief executive, the successful application by Geoff Dudman, the council's conservation officer, to secure the pavilion a Grade I listing marked a turning point. Not only was the building now recognized nationally as being of special architectural and historic importance, but any council proposals to modify it would have to undergo lengthy, and much more public, scrutiny.

However, while the listing might have halted any further insensitive modifications, there remained the far more difficult questions of how the building could effectively be repaired and restored, and, importantly, who or what was going to pay for it all. Rother was still short of money, the pavilion was still rotting, and now even the simplest of repairs would be subject to exacting processes of consultation with outside authorities before anything could be touched. Powell identified the solution of establishing a separate trust that could work with the council for the building's conservation and also access funds from charities and other funding bodies in ways impossible for any local authority. The seeds of the future Pavilion Trust had been sown.

Left By the time restoration began in the 1990s, the pavilion was looking shabby and neglected.

The trust's genesis was not immediate. In 1987 an exhibition was organized by the independent architecture magazine *A3 Times* to celebrate the centenary of Erich Mendelsohn. It opened, fittingly, with his finest British project, the De La Warr Pavilion. At the exhibition launch a number of the building's supporters met Cyril Sweett, Mendelsohn's original quantity surveyor, who instantly offered to help.

It took more than a year to set the ball in motion, but in March 1989 a small band of just fifteen supporters — councillors and public alike — met in the pavilion's foyer to establish formally the new trust. Sweett had also managed to enlist some powerful patrons to the cause, among them Sir Hugh Casson, the former president of the Royal Academy and provost of the Royal College of Art; Sir Denys Lasdun, architect of the National Theatre; and Lord Rayne, one of the National Theatre's board members and chairman of London Merchant Securities. To these were added the names of the 11th Earl De La Warr, grandson of the building's founder, and Esther Mendelsohn Joseph, the architect's daughter. There was much to do, and with its new chairman, Peter Evenden, a local chartered building surveyor, and three further committee members — Don Kimber, who succeeded Evenden in 1991, and Councillors Christine Bayliss and Jill Theis — the new trust immediately set to work.

From the outset, the trust had three distinct aims. First, to achieve the building's restoration by funding specific, achievable refurbishment projects and ensuring that a wider restoration programme was carried out sensitively. Second, to promote knowledge and understanding of the building, its architecture and its history by working with schools, colleges and universities. Third, to campaign in order to raise the profile of the building and win recognition of it as both a national and an international landmark. The trust promptly set about attaining the first of these goals.

Although the council could never be accused of neglecting the building, hitherto repairs and modifications had tended to be undertaken piecemeal, as funds became available. The hurricane

Above Initial work on the terraces rapidly unearthed serious decay to the building's fabric.

that hit the south of England in October 1987 badly damaged the auditorium roof and, with no money available to repair it immediately, the council had little option but to close the auditorium for a prolonged period. In 1989 cracks emerged in the building's south elevation, so the council commissioned a structural survey to identify the root of the problem. Worried that this might set off another round of potentially damaging modifications, the trust proposed instead that an external firm of architects undertake a comprehensive study in order to map out a strategic direction for the building that could then inform both its redevelopment and the restoration work needed to achieve it. The council rejected the idea and instructed its own borough architect to start work immediately on major repairs to the building's balconies and south elevation. Undeterred, the trust went ahead with the development of its own strategy, appointing the emerging practice of architects Troughton McAslan to undertake an initial appraisal and formulate a long-term restoration and usage plan for the pavilion, presented in a comprehensive strategy report. While the practice was preparing its report, the trust also started work on its educational programme, initiating a series of talks on the building for local residents, producing an educational pack for schools, and launching a newsletter for its growing band of members.

It was the visit to the building by Peter Palumbo, the outspoken chairman of the Arts Council, that really put the trust's work on the map. Agreeing to write a foreword to the trust's strategy report of 1990, he exhorted the council to take its findings on board: "The local authority, struggling to maintain a building it commissioned and now owns, has neither the means nor the expertise to carry out urgent remedial work." Significantly, he added: "A complete review and audit of the pavilion's current use, including its artistic policy and marketing strategy ... will help make sense of the architectural restoration and improvements which are envisaged." At last, the council took heed. Following elections in 1991, the new Liberal Democrat administration finally agreed, in 1992, to accept the Pavilion Trust's approach to the building, including its new Stage 1 restoration strategy report, and appointed John McAslan of Troughton McAslan to oversee the building's future restoration.

The practice's report set the tone for the coming years. For the first time, the large number of alterations and modifications to the building's interior were chronicled, supporting the practice's case for all future work to adopt a strategic, planned approach – one driven not only by conservation concerns but also by the needs of the building's modern uses, whatever they might be. Importantly, the report's argument for the preparation of a long-term strategy for the pavilion centred on strengthening its arts programme, creating a new audience, and raising funds for a 'pilot project' to demonstrate that the building's transformation was underway. The report also highlighted one of the key problems that the council had faced: namely, that in order to operate effectively, the building always seemed to need more space. Hitherto, rather than tackle this matter head on, the council had tried to reshape the internal arrangement of the building. The architects proposed that a two-storey extension be added to the building's north wall, an idea first mooted by Maxwell Fry nearly thirty years previously. Ultimately, the extension as proposed by McAslan was not built. However, the architects' approach sufficiently impressed the council to lead it to halt the works being undertaken by the borough architects and instead commission the practice to oversee the entire restoration of the south elevation, the balconies of which were, by now, badly in need of attention. Furthermore, the council agreed to contribute some £900,000 towards the works.

Meanwhile, Palumbo was in the process of establishing a special architecture unit at the Arts Council, and his support for the pavilion had strengthened the case for its restoration work to be grant-assisted by English Heritage, the government-sponsored body established in 1983 to maintain the nation's historic environment. English Heritage had first been brought into the frame in 1992, when the Pavilion Trust secured its financial support for a second-stage strategy report it was planning to commission from Troughton McAslan. Having agreed to part-fund the strategy, it was therefore a natural step for English Heritage to then become more closely involved in funding the actual restoration works, and it agreed to do so in December that year. This was just as well: the initial repairs to the building's terrace revealed far worse decay than had at first been anticipated, so costs were sure to rise.

McAslan was also concerned that insufficient care was being given to the techniques involved in the work initially commissioned by the council's architects. The borough's approach had recommended that, once stripped away and repaired, the building's structural columns should be fireproofed by coating them with retardant paint, casing them with fibreglass and applying ceramic tiles on top. Seeking a second opinion, McAslan brought in the engineering firm F.J. Samuely and Partners. The company's founder, Felix Samuely, had been the pavilion's structural engineer. Samuely and Partners advised a different approach. While the council's proposed technique might work for a while, it said, the extremes of heat and cold the building suffered each year would soon make the tiles crack and loosen. For longevity, it would be better to pump the hollow steel columns with concrete, which would maintain their original, slim shape while also fireproofing them satisfactorily.

Now that Troughton McAslan was in charge of the immediate restoration works, it seemed only sensible that the practice should look at other aspects of the building's requirements. As a result, late in 1992 the council commissioned it to conduct a complete survey of the pavilion to phase future restoration works, charting the dilapidation and suggesting repairs required both inside and out, including the building's internal fixtures and fittings, its environmental services and its complex internal works. The survey report was published in May 1993. The same month, restoration of the south terrace was completed. It turned out that the balconies had needed to be almost totally rebuilt and the rotting steel columns stripped back and repaired, or new steels inserted and then retiled in a similar vein to the original designs. New paving was also laid, since the original terrace tiling had become badly worn and cracked by having had heavy windscreens on castors dragged across it since the 1960s. For the first time since before the war, the building was looking clean and elegant once more.

The trust was also hard at work. With the new, agreed strategy in place, it could start work on the other features of its restoration programme, tackling specific, practical projects of its own. In 1992 it launched the first of a series of successful fundraising campaigns to restore several of the pavilion's less structural, more visible, features. With the support of Ann, Countess De La Warr, the 11th Earl's wife, the trust launched a £20,000 campaign to restore the building's flagpole (located above its north staircase), repair Mendelsohn's famous chrome light fitting descending through the south staircase, and replace the building's stylish roundel nameplates, which had disappeared during the war. By the following year, sufficient funds had been found to restore the flagpole and start work on the light fitting. The fitting had been covered with thick blue paint in the 1960s to reduce the need for cleaning. The paint had to be painstakingly stripped away to reveal the gleaming chrome beneath. Funding for the roundels took longer to secure and ultimately required some £35,000, but the trust's determination never ceased, and the roundels were finally reinstated in 1997.

Meanwhile, the trust was gearing up its educational activities. In 1992 a successful artist- and architect-in-residence project was launched to work with local primary schoolchildren and students from the nearby sixth-form college in order to widen their awareness of the built environment and work on a number of projects related to the pavilion and its restoration. The following year, a wider education project was established, run in conjunction with the Construction Industry Training Board, which developed a resource pack for schools linked to the National Curriculum. Many schools were involved in workshops, seminars and exhibitions, ultimately leading the trust to arrange for an education room to be established on the first floor of the building for the use of visiting schools, colleges and researchers.

In 1994 another campaign was launched, this time to restore the building's famed furniture. A hidden cache of the chairs and tables by Alvar Aalto, badly damaged, had been discovered in 1992 in an upstairs storeroom. They were all carefully reconditioned over the following decade, with each item of furniture being 'sponsored' by a donor to have the paint stripped off, the bentwood timber frames repaired, and the blue or vermilion seats and cream table tops restored. By 2002 the trust had managed to restore no fewer than twelve chairs, fifteen tables and two stools in this way, once more reinstating a key feature of the original decor of the pavilion.

While individual restoration projects did much to help the look of the building, the future purpose of the pavilion remained unclear. The council faced several options: it could sell the building, thereby freeing itself of its costly maintenance responsibilities but potentially undermining its desire to provide entertainment for the population; or it could diversify the pavilion's activities, moving the pavilion more into the area of mass-market leisure, although this might threaten the building's architectural heritage. Or the council could continue to fund the pavilion's tactical maintenance programme while retaining the same mix of facilities and entertainment. None of the choices was straightforward. The trust's position was clear: nothing short of complete restoration and preservation in a sustainable way for the benefit of the public was acceptable.

To help resolve the dilemma, the Pavilion Trust had been putting together funding to commission a second strategy report, this time to develop proposals for fundraising and the future management and interior restoration of the building. By 1993 the funding was in place from English Heritage, the council and a series of other bodies, and Troughton McAslan was commissioned to produce Stage II of the building's restoration strategy. The council itself also commissioned consultants to look at development options for the pavilion's future use. Until this time, the pavilion had focused primarily on entertainment and catering services. The consultants' report highlighted the pavilion's potential as a "living art gallery" that, given the management and marketing resources, could develop a higher profile for the arts. The report also suggested, for the first time, that the pavilion might transfer its ownership to an independent charitable trust, enabling it to embark on a fundraising strategy that could lead to the building's full restoration and refurbishment and secure its future operation.

The fact that the two reports coincided was crucial. Having conducted the major restoration of the exterior, McAslan, in his new report, set out proposals to restore some of the original spaces to the building's much-altered interior, the most important of

Above, top and bottom The renamed Elizabeth room enclosed the sun parlour, merged it with the reading room, and added carpets and curtains to screen off areas.

these being work to the building's first floor, by then a patchwork of makeshift meeting rooms, dowdy bars and garish function suites. Restoring the original space and dimensions would also allow the building's new function to flourish; the "living art gallery" could become real. As a result, in 1994 the second major phase of the pavilion's restoration got underway, with the false ceiling of the gloomy Edinburgh room being stripped away and the room once more restored to Mendelsohn's original design for the lecture theatre – only this time its folding screen doors would open into a bright new space for art exhibitions. The 1960s panelled bar was removed, the carpet replaced with cork tiling and new bent-plywood furniture purchased from Finmar, the same company that had supplied the originals. The Elizabeth room was dismantled, too, its corrugated ceiling torn down to reveal north-facing windows and the original paintwork, with the whole room being restored to provide a far brighter, more flexible space for functions and entertainment.

By 1995 more than £1,500,000 had been spent on the restoration works, more than £270,000 of which had come from the Pavilion Trust, much of it through two major grants from the European Union in Brussels and the Getty Grant Program in Los Angeles. The grants had been identified by Peter Evenden, now the trust's energetic treasurer, and by John McAslan, and secured through his practice's endeavours. In addition to adopting a more strategic approach towards restoration, Rother Council began to make changes in the way the pavilion was managed, appointing its first marketing officer at the pavilion and commissioning a fundraising strategy from an independent consultant. For the first time, a real picture of the pavilion's theatre attendance numbers and the demographics of the primary catchment area had emerged, and, together with a wider consultation through visitor surveys, the council now had the necessary information to figure out existing visitor patterns and to plot ways to attract new audiences.

Research indicated that Bexhill itself was undergoing demographic change, and that the pavilion was under-exploited. Although used frequently by local older people, holiday visitors and coach

Above The first stage of the restoration works inside the building returned the space to its original dimensions, let in light from ceiling height and transformed it into a gallery space.

Below The first-floor bar had become home to decoration of every kind, with carpet, patterned wallpaper and tinsel at Christmas.

Bottom Restoration has returned the space to a clean, open and bright area, more in keeping with the original designs.

parties, it was grossly under-used by other groups within the immediate catchment area, particularly by families, younger people and those with an interest in the arts as opposed to seaside entertainment. Coupled with the demand for good catering and retail facilities, catering consultants had advised of the need to move away from the existing cafeteria-type trade and into a more upmarket café/bistro enterprise. Research into national trends in leisure activities showed a growing market for the visual arts and increasing attendance figures for well-run and imaginative museums and art galleries. In addition, an increasing interest in the art, design and architecture of the Modernist period was emerging, as was an expanding market for short-break holidays for domestic and European visitors. And there was more. Consultation with such regional stakeholders as the Arts Council and Tourism South East and specialists in a variety of arts and tourism fields showed a gap in regional provision for the visual arts and a significant potential market for a centre focused on art and architecture in a uniquely apt setting. The pavilion fitted this role perfectly. With support from the Arts Council and the Pavilion Trust, debate around the pavilion's role as an arts-focused initiative began to escalate, culminating in 1995 in an arts strategy devised by Rother Council. This strategy saw the visual arts as an effective way forward for both the town and the De La Warr Pavilion.

The pavilion's sixtieth-birthday celebrations in December 1995 provided proof that the trust, the pavilion's management and the council were all now working along similar lines. The pavilion had organized a major exhibition in its new gallery space of the work of Connell, Ward & Lucas, the influential 1930s Modernist architectural practice, together with lectures by the architect Dennis Sharp, who had designed and curated the exhibition. The trust, for its part, organized a sixtieth-anniversary party, combining it with a science and technology challenge workshop for local schoolchildren, and invited the architect's daughter, Esther Mendelsohn Joseph, and the 11th Earl and Countess De La Warr to be guests of honour. To conclude events, on the actual anniversary of the pavilion's inauguration, Rother Council organized a gala concert by the Bournemouth Symphony Orchestra, together with a civic reception to mark the recently completed restoration works.

"It was Esther", says McAslan, "who would inspire us all to continue our endeavours to restore her father's great project in England. She introduced me to many of her father's former colleagues, people such as the remarkable Julius Posener in Berlin, and she encouraged me to lecture wherever I could find an audience interested to hear about the De La Warr. My family became firm friends with Esther, as well as her daughter Daria and her family, and we spent many happy times in the mid- to late 1990s at her home in San Francisco, with its marvellous arts collection, much of it focused on Erich Mendelsohn's work."

In November 1995 Anthony Leonard, the council's new, forward-thinking director of community services, developed an ambitious £8,900,000 plan for a large-scale redevelopment of the pavilion as a visual arts and architecture centre, and put the proposals forward to the Arts Council Lottery. Although the bid was not initially granted, the Arts Council did grant Rother Council £500,000 in 1996 to develop the plan further and launch future fundraising. Particular encouragement was given at the time to the development of the existing theatre as well as the initiatives in visual arts and architecture. It was clear that the new ideas were bearing fruit.

For the Pavilion Trust, a campaigner from the sidelines for so long, the Arts Council's award also marked a new period of far closer co-operation with the authorities it had sought to influence over the years. At the pavilion, the council had taken on a new general manager, Caroline Collier, in 1996 to carry the work forward and, together, the trust and the new administration developed an extensive programme of work across education, campaigning and fundraising. While the council was developing its large-scale proposals for the building's future, the trust worked on smaller but highly visible fundraising campaigns. Design workshops for schools were held at the building in conjunction with RIBA South East; a programme of guided tours was developed, and talks and lectures for groups were organized. Local residents' past recollections of the building were recorded by a trust committee member, and a comprehensive archive of books, photographs and designs of the building was put together, located in the education room as a resource for future generations. The trust commissioned a book, *Bucking the Trend* (2001), compiled by the author of this publication, Alastair Fairley, profiling the life and times of the 9th Earl De La Warr. In 1998 it successfully raised £12,000 to purchase the original sketch Edward Wadsworth had produced for his enormous mural, thus reuniting the two for the first time since the mural was completed. That same year, the trust also launched what was to become its biggest and most successful appeal, to raise £75,000 to replace the building's 1970s bandstand.

There remained one last battle for the pavilion to be fought, and this time it struck at the very heart of the building's *raison d'être*. Within a year of its original 1996 Arts Lottery award, a new, more ambitious scheme for the pavilion's redevelopment had been formulated by Caroline Collier, John McAslan + Partners (as the practice became known in 1996) under the leadership of McAslan and his partner, Adam Brown, and the council's tourism and leisure team, led by Anthony Leonard. In all, £16,500,000 was being sought to transform the building into a centre for art, architecture and live performance. With the backing of both the Rother councillors and English Heritage, the bid was finally submitted to the Arts Council Lottery at the start of 1998. Tense months followed. Plans were amended, listed-building consent sought and planning approval obtained, all in the hope and expectation that, finally, the building's future would be secured. But times had moved on: as administrator of the Arts Lottery, the Arts Council was reviewing its own operating strategy. The way the Arts Lottery funds were used to support large-scale capital projects was, similarly, under review, a process influenced in no small way by public outcry at the huge sums provided by the Lottery to the redevelopment of the Royal Opera House in Covent Garden, London.

Below A key part of the final programme of restoration, the auditorium has new seating and improved lighting suitable for modern performance.

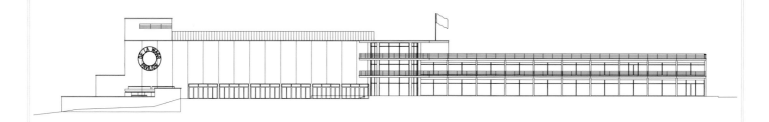

The decision in 1999 not to grant the latest Lottery bid was announced by the Arts Council the day before the government's culture secretary, Chris Smith, was due to visit the pavilion, a coincidence that did little to soothe the sore disappointment in Bexhill. Yet, even then, all was not lost. The Arts Lottery offered the project £120,000 to reformulate or revise the pavilion's Lottery application. Based on the Lottery's view that such major development of the auditorium was not justified and that the need for the pavilion's restoration was as much a heritage issue as an arts one, meetings were arranged to discuss a possible approach by Rother to both the Arts Lottery and the Heritage Lottery in the future. Rother Council, too, was bullish – at first. Following on from the aim set out in the 1995 Lottery bid that the pavilion should have a role as a resource of local, national and international importance, it identified sufficient funds to undertake much-needed repairs and refurbishment of the auditorium and also finally tackle repairs to the hall's roof, which had been damaged in the hurricane more than ten years before.

The elections of May 1999, however, brought in a new, Conservative council, the members of which expressed renewed concerns over both the continuing necessity of repairs to the building and its increased running costs, which contributed to an annual burden on local ratepayers of almost £1,000,000. Perhaps the private sector, the councillors argued, could offer a

solution. Rother's officers were appointed to find out, and invited expressions of interest in a private and public partnership with the council "for the continuing refurbishment and operation of the Pavilion". The national press decried the proposal, with *The Observer* asking "Will the barbarians triumph at Bexhill?" and the *Daily Telegraph* announcing "Shame and scandal at Bexhill". News had leaked out that one of the companies that had approached Rother was the pub chain J.D. Wetherspoon. Incensed residents wrote to the *Bexhill Observer*. The Pavilion Trust – with its campaign entitled 'Public house or public amenity?' – rallied the troops. Protests were organized at council meetings; five thousand residents signed a petition opposing the plans; letters were dispatched to architects, politicians and other key allies.

In November 1999 Alan Haydon was appointed director of the pavilion, with the task of developing its arts programming alongside a fresh approach to Lottery funding, in parallel to the council's private-sector plans. At the same time, the Arts Lottery Board advised that it had 'ring-fenced' £4,100,000 in support of a redevelopment strategy driven by the visual arts.

By March 2000 the campaign against private–public partnership was in full swing. During a visit to the pavilion that month, Arts Minister Alan Howarth said he was "strongly opposed" to turning the building over to a commercial concern. Richard Rogers and

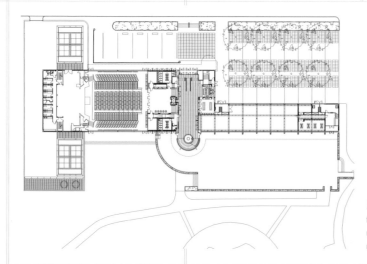

Left John McAslan + Partners' site plan shows two new wings to the north and south of the restored pavilion that accommodate much-needed office space and rehearsal studios.

Opposite John McAslan + Partners'
remodelled pavilion uses the site's natural
slope to minimize the visual impact of the
new additions.

Below Even from the air, the pavilion has
a distinctive footprint, although trees and
gravel have given way to more uniform
car parking.

Denys Lasdun wrote to the national press. Even Queen Elizabeth the Queen Mother contributed to the debate, writing to ask the council what its intentions were for the building she had opened in 1935. Pressure was mounting from all sides. Peter Ainsworth, the shadow culture secretary, toured the building, pointing out to Rother's Conservative council leader, Ivor Brampton, that "tourism, arts and leisure are the fastest-growing areas of economic regeneration today". The television company Channel 4 produced a stinging attack on the proposals in a documentary by architect Piers Gough. And in September 2000 Marcus Binney, writing in *The Times*, decried the plans, stating that "Half the towns of Europe now dream of building a modern masterpiece like the Bilbao Guggenheim. Amazingly, sedate Bexhill achieved this 65 years ago" (19 September 2000, section 2, pp. 14–16). By October 2000 Rother's councillors had dropped the investigation into a private-sector partnership and agreed to pursue proposals that Alan Haydon and his team had developed, together with funding applications to the Arts Lottery and the Heritage Lottery. At last, the bid proved successful. In April 2002, the Arts Council announced it would commit £4,100,000 towards the restoration, with a further £1,900,000 being provided by the Heritage Lottery Fund.

With funding now obtained to complete the pavilion's restoration, and recognition of the building's place in international architecture secured, the aims of the Pavilion Trust had been achieved. In 2002, thirteen years after its inauguration, the trust agreed to cease operating. In its stead, a new charity had been established – the De La Warr Pavilion Charitable Trust – which in time would assume ownership of the building and run its programme, finally freeing Rother Council from the responsibility of maintaining the pavilion, both physically and artistically.

Although the building's future was assured financially, the doubts that had erupted in 2000 over its ownership had delayed other projects, particularly the construction of the new bandstand. The bandstand development had been different from the outset. Niall McLaughlin, who had won the Young British Architect of the Year award shortly after winning the trust's competition (initiated by John McAslan and the RIBA), had established a close working

relationship not only with his team of builders, structural engineers and junior architects, but also with a twenty-four-strong team of local schoolchildren. Throughout 2001 the schoolchildren returned to the project, taking part in design days and workshops, learning engineering and construction techniques, building models and coming up with design and engineering ideas, many of which were integrated into the finished product by the architects.

In December 2001, just four months before the formal announcement of the Lottery award, the first physical signs of the pavilion's remarkable renaissance were revealed, as the building's extraordinary new bandstand was hoisted into position, its wave-like fibreglass and plywood roof floating like a seagull in the wind. The accolades were swift in coming. Within months, McLaughlin's design had won a highly coveted RIBA award, and the education programme he had managed was adopted by the sponsor, the Construction Industry Training Board, for use by schools nationwide as a module for teaching design and technology.

By 2004 it was time for the redevelopment and restoration itself to get under way. In the years John McAslan had been involved in the project, his architectural practice had grown into one of international significance, remodelling a number of Modernist buildings, including Charles Rennie Mackintosh's final work, at 78 Derngate in Northampton, and Frank Lloyd Wright's Florida

Southern College, as well as designing major new works in the United Kingdom and overseas. McAslan's initial proposals for the pavilion's restoration, which had been put forward to the Lottery in 2001, had sought to undertake much of the work without the need to close the pavilion to the public completely, but costs and safety concerns meant that this was not possible. By closing the building to the public, however, work could be done far more quickly. McAslan + Partners' approach has been essentially to restore the pavilion as faithfully as possible to the original concepts of Mendelsohn's design, while satisfactorily meeting the clear requirement for additional space and facilities to cater for the building's future use. As a result, the pavilion is closer now than at any time since the 1930s to the simple yet enchanting design first opened to an expectant public seventy years ago.

In their restoration work, the architects have stripped away many of the alterations or additions made to the pavilion over the decades, bringing light once more into the building, while also returning many of the rooms or spaces to their original, balanced dimensions. For example, the relocation of the lift, towards the south end of the main entrance hall, has enabled Mendelsohn's original design for the auditorium foyer, with its doors opening on to an impressive room, to be recaptured. Similarly, the introduction of alarmed fire screens to the main entrance meant that the heavy fire doors erected there in the 1970s could be removed, with the

Left Restoration also brought backstage dressing rooms up to a higher standard in order to accommodate visiting touring companies.

Below The wave-like bandstand has received awards from the RIBA for its innovative design.

Left Architects and students watch the new bandstand being lifted into place in 2001.

entrance doors now opening directly into the stunning main foyer. The sun parlour, one of the most short-lived features of the original design, has been restored once more, this time to seat the visitors eating at the bistro located on the restored first floor. The roof is now open to the public once again, the siting of a fire escape leading down to the sun parlour enabling it to be used as exhibition space.

The major structural work has focused on the auditorium backstage area, where the original steel windows have been reinstated and further repair work to the roof completed, although the new lift shaft and fire escape on the roof also required careful structural interventions to the building's original frame. A large plant room has also had to be dug under the north car park to house bulky air-conditioning equipment required to service the new gallery.

The original architects' attention to detail has been followed. Timber-framed windows, installed as cheaper alternatives to their rusting predecessors during the 1960s and 1970s, have been replaced with steel frames, painted with rust-resistant paint, and faithfully reglazed. The scored, battered windscreens on the south terrace have been replaced with more sympathetic glass substitutes. Cracks and glazing in the external Cullamix render have been hacked away and filled, and the whole building cleaned and repainted. Even the heavy main entrance doors,

so long the subject of complaint by visitors struggling to open them, have been replaced with identical copies supported by counterbalances to make them easier to open.

Internally, rooms have been returned to their original shape and size, although the new uses to which they are being put demonstrate the flexibility of the pavilion's original design. Most significant is the creation of the pavilion's new ground-floor gallery. With its neat arrangement of roller blinds housed against double-glazed panels, the gallery is now one of the largest and most fully equipped in the region and meets the environmental conditions required to attract exhibitions of international acclaim, a key aim of the refurbishment strategy. The huge expanses of glass are treated with special filters to reduce solar gain and damaging ultraviolet light, while the deep terrace above also shades the room from the harsh midday sunlight. The floor is of white oak. The room may no longer be a cafeteria and restaurant, but it has the same open feel of the original design.

Upstairs, the visual arts function continues, with refurbished gallery spaces now provided on both the first and second floors, together with yet more exhibition space on the roof. The pavilion also includes a bar, café and restaurant on the first floor, and a shop on the ground floor, adjoining the open-plan information and booking desk leading off the main entrance lobby.

That these new facilities could be so easily accommodated is the result of two new additions to the pavilion's overall plan. The first of these, to the south-west of the auditorium, is a new wing for the pavilion's staff, including toilets, changing facilities, kitchens, meeting rooms and offices accommodating up to twenty people. A near-identical extension, to the north of the west wing, provides a dedicated space for education and community activities and rehearsal and studio space, again with its own toilets, kitchen and storeroom, which allow the facility to be used independently of the main pavilion at any time. But, like Mendelsohn before him, McAslan has sought to use the natural slope of the site to good effect, sinking the rooms partially below ground level, both to minimize their impact when viewed from the seafront and to maintain the symmetry of the western elevation.

Seventy years after its first opening, the pavilion is once again receiving plaudits from the architectural world for its design. That it still functions in the same way it did in 1935 is a testament not only to the skill of its original architects, but also to the dedication over the years of its staff, supporters and former and present owners. Although the pavilion is an icon of another era, its survival and renewed vigour serve to demonstrate the merit of that period's principles of design, social advancement and enlightenment.

chapter 9 a building for the future
alan haydon

This book reflects upon the architectural and social history surrounding the De La Warr Pavilion. It tells of the climate in which the building was created, its heyday during the 1930s, the financial struggles over its maintenance and the ever-changing debate as to its purpose. Importantly, the story illustrates the frequent attempts to 'improve' the building in order for it to reflect these changing opinions relating to its purpose. This closing chapter seeks to highlight the pavilion's more recent history, which has helped give rise to its physical and cultural renewal.

The story suggests that, except in its early years, the pavilion never quite achieved or sustained the cultural ambitions for which it was conceived. In part, history gives its reasons: politics, war and economic hardship had a direct impact on the building's fate for several decades. However, the story also reflects two distinct reactions to the pavilion's architecture and, importantly, to its function. On the one hand, we read of the appreciation of the brave architectural gesture the pavilion made and of the attempts by its owners in the pre-war years to deliver an equally challenging artistic programme. On the other hand, we learn of critics' disapproval that the pavilion ever took shape in the first place. As time passed, there was equal disdain for the service it offered to the local community. It was as if the aspirations of its public were not in harmony with what the owners of the pavilion were seeking to achieve for the long-term benefit of a town in need of rejuvenation.

Such debate has continued for the past seventy years with various outcomes, most of which did no more than assist the building's general path of both physical and spiritual decline. Today, however, at the start of the new millennium, not only has the physical well-being of the pavilion been addressed, but a new cultural and social identity, perhaps echoing the spirit in which it was created, has been developed.

The background to this most recent episode in the pavilion's history has been complex and challenging. While the need to restore the building's fabric was generally acknowledged, the question of the pavilion's purpose was more difficult, particularly if its administrators were to avoid repeating previous attempts at refurbishment without a strong sense of purpose. At the same time, the town of Bexhill was again concerned that its own future could be realized only through the process of regeneration and that, perhaps once more, the pavilion could be the catalyst for such a change.

For the pavilion to be such a catalyst, a vision of its future had to be created by its new independent administration long before the case could be made to secure the necessary resources to meet the building's urgent physical need of repair. This new administration, under the stewardship of a charitable trust, had to determine a means by which it could finally bring a world-class programme to a world-class building. This was the greater challenge: to

reinterpret for the modern day the ambitions for which the pavilion was created and to secure a more cohesive identity that connected the arts to the broader cultural and social environment. Part of this challenge, alongside the issue of securing the financial means by which work could begin, was to develop a new kind of cultural programme that acknowledged the De La Warr Pavilion's historical context but went further towards meeting the aspirations of a changing twenty-first-century community.

The unpacking of history, along with the readiness to respond to new ideas and challenges, helped the administration determine a clear set of objectives. One of the key principles was to challenge people's perceptions of contemporary art and, in so doing, change attitudes towards the arts in the long term. To achieve this, the administration placed education at the heart of its programming philosophy by forming relationships with artists, allowing them to create new experiences for their audiences, and, importantly, by treating the pavilion as a place for inspiring creativity and the production of new work. The administration was also keen that the collaborative spirit that originally brought the pavilion's architects together with such artists and designers as László Moholy-Nagy, Alvar Aalto, Frank Dobson and Edward Wadsworth should be reignited. Such direct engagement with artists as a means of creating programmes that would have meaning for both the place and the people was fundamental to its approach.

With new ideas having been introduced in the late 1990s, the new millennium presented the opportunity to follow through these principles in new programming initiatives, and to begin to signal future aspirations in the hope of securing the necessary capital investment.

The year 2000 was, among other things, the Arts Council's designated Year of the Artist, and, in response, the pavilion invited the artist Ian Breakwell to work on a project about the enigmatic qualities of the building, its sea views and its visitors, and to consider creative ideas that the experience might inspire. Breakwell focused on the building's architecture, its quality of light and the patterns of behaviour of its visitors, and in 2002 his experiences became the subject of his film *The Other Side*.

Breakwell observed older people attending afternoon dances at the pavilion and then went on to study the behaviour of others on the beach nearby, particularly the town's youths. His film depicted people on the pavilion's balcony dancing to the haunting music of Schubert, but ended abruptly with the sound of breaking glass and the thunderous crashing of waves and gathering of storm clouds. The work, which was projected on both sides of a wall constructed in the centre of the pavilion gallery, suggested the turning of the tide from one reality to another. The difference was stark, with the dancers' nostalgic happiness and sense

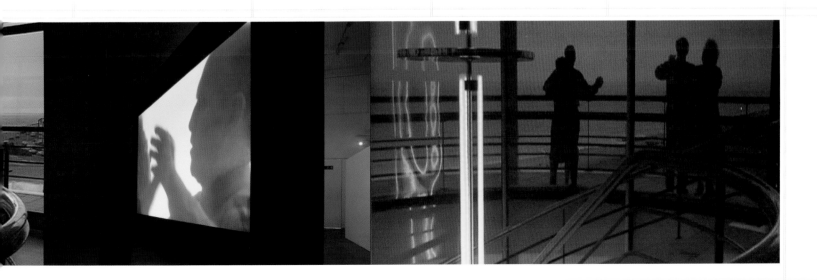

of indifference to the world around them contrasted with teenage boredom and disaffection.

The success of *The Other Side* can be measured in several ways. When the film was first shown, the response among local people – particularly among those associated with its subject matter – was emotional applause. There was substantial coverage in the national press, and as a result of a visit by Sir Nicholas Serota, the director of Tate, the work was purchased for its collection, and was shown at Tate Britain during 2004. *The Other Side* has thus been an important commission for the De La Warr Pavilion as well as a seminal work for the artist.

A number of important exhibitions took place over the four-year period leading up to the redevelopment in 2004 that similarly focused on the work of individual artists and their responses to the architecture and setting of the pavilion. Some common threads ran through the different artists' presentations. The cubic white space of the first-floor gallery, and the natural light that enters through the eastern clerestory windows, together with the borrowed light from the south-facing floor-to-ceiling windows beyond the gallery itself, create different experiences of place for both artist and viewer. The movement of the shifting light in the space in accordance with the time of day and seasonal change casts shadows across the walls that themselves become an integral part of

the work in the gallery and contribute to the experience of the exhibition installation overall.

For Antoni Malinowski, the ever-present seascape and the mercurial quality of the light within the gallery provided inspiration for his site-specific installation in 2001. Tracking the movement of light across the space by 'drawing' directly on to the north wall with threads of black bitumen, he encapsulated a moment in time for the viewer to experience.

The fusion of architecture, light and the particularities of the pavilion have continued to have an important influence on the exhibition programme. The pavilion has also established partnerships with a number of similar organizations, including the Estorick Foundation in London, the Laboratory at the Ruskin School of Drawing and Fine Art at the University of Oxford, Film and Video Umbrella in London, and Photoworks in Brighton.

Over this period, such artists as John Riddy, Stephen Hughes and Michael Danner showed new portfolios of photographic work. For the artist Mario Rossi, the space allowed for the full presentation in 2000 of a body of one hundred works taken from the final frames of films depicting the words 'The End'. Boyd Webb's response in 2002 was to make a short film, *Horse and Dog*, featuring two clumsy pantomime characters on a camping trip. The film depicted

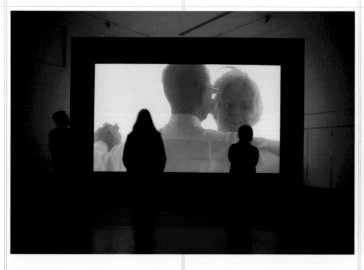

two animals acting out human role-play, imitating the characteristic behaviour of the seaside holidaymaker.

In 2003 the Norwegian artist Kjell Torriset responded to an invitation to create and present a new body of work that would be his first solo exhibition in the United Kingdom. Widely known in Norway and other Scandinavian countries, Torriset, who works from his studios nearby in St Leonards, created more than three hundred paintings, hung from floor to ceiling in a grid formation around three walls of the gallery. The exhibition not only challenged the perception of what painting can be, but pushed the boundaries of how space can be used and how the fusion of both painting and space can create an exciting experience.

Exhibitions of a more thematic nature also came into play within the broader programming context, responding to either seasons of activity or specific events. Furthering the administration's wish to engage with ideas from artists living and working in the local area, and following an exhibition of the artist's work at the pavilion in 2001, Colin Booth's exhibition *Colour White* came to fruition in 2002. It focused on artists' interest in the properties of the colour white, including its complexity and the means by which it reflects and absorbs light and highlights surface, texture, space and form. The exhibition featured work by Ben Nicholson and Naum Gabo, alongside such contemporary artists as Anish Kapoor, Lolly Batty,

Simon Callery, A.K. Dolven, Callum Innes, Langlands and Bell, and Jason Martin.

During this period, and in keeping with the principle that education, in its broadest sense, was at the heart of the pavilion's vision, a strategy was introduced to engage new audiences by establishing long-term relationships with communities that had otherwise been excluded from the pavilion's *raison d'être*. In tandem with a new approach to Christmas entertainment, the organization chose to break from the traditional, populist mould of pantomime, introducing instead a quality production to appeal to a wider family audience. To this end, the pavilion presented productions of the Royal Shakespeare Company's *The Wizard of Oz* in 2001, followed by *Peter Pan*, also by the RSC, in 2002. These productions not only proved successful in attracting larger audiences than ever before, but also gave the pavilion the opportunity to put on exhibitions that explored themes within the shows. For example, *AKA*, an exhibition presented at the same time as the *Wizard of Oz* production, explored the concept of disguise and role-play. The work of such artists as Cindy Sherman, Gavin Turk and Paul M. Smith was included, as was Man Ray's enigmatic photograph of Marcel Duchamp portraying the character Rrose Sélavy. The show *Peter Pan* offered the opportunity to present in 2002 a solo exhibition of recent work by Laura Ford that had previously been shown in Salamanca in

Below, top Kjell Torriset's installation in 2003 filled Gallery 2 with more than three hundred individual paintings.

Below, centre Antoni Malinowski's installation in 2001 responded to the extraordinary light that now filters through the clerestory windows of Gallery 2.

Bottom Stephen Hughes's 2001 exhibition featured photographs of places on the fringes of urban and natural landscapes.

Spain as part of the city's European Capital of Culture celebrations. The exhibition featured life-sized sculptures of reindeer alongside subversive child-like figures in military colours, evoking the deeper meanings of Pan and his cohorts.

The year 2000 saw a challenge to the pavilion's traditional programme of outdoor summer activities. Audiences had previously been entertained with brass bands and puppet shows that maintained the notion of seaside tradition without offering anything more creative or ground-breaking. *Jour de Fête* was conceived as a challenging, high-energy, culturally diverse and explicitly entertaining programme that delivered the unexpected to its audience. It was a mixture of new circus, sculpture, comedy and thought-provoking performance that aimed to inspire laughter, shock and amazement in its onlookers and participants. The finale was a visual spectacular, exploiting the building as backdrop, prop and subject matter.

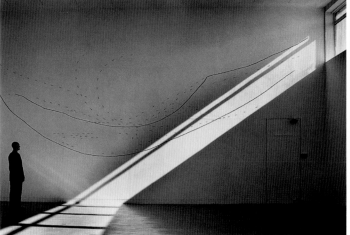

The now firmly established *Jour de Fête* programme has developed significantly over a five-year period, with such companies as Walk the Plank, Avanti Display, Les Grooms and Mischief Le Bas presenting newly commissioned pieces and attracting audiences in their thousands. For the town, *Jour de Fête* has become part of its new identity; for the pavilion, it has established a new and continually changing tradition.

Within the sphere of live performance, the artistic programme also aimed to inject change, and to offer new things to new audiences. To this end, new relationships were formed with contemporary dance companies, theatre companies presenting new writing, and orchestras wishing to offer a more challenging repertoire of music. Audiences responded in various ways. With some productions, the risk paid off; with others, the challenge was too great. However, with balance and careful marketing, the core audience remained loyal and slowly grew in size, range and enthusiasm. New audiences, particularly of young people and families, also began to emerge. Memorable successes included productions from the companies Knee High, Out of Joint and Random Dance.

Prior to the pavilion's closure in 2004 and in readiness for its redevelopment, the framework for both the reopening programme and, within obvious constraints, a 'without walls' calendar of events and initiatives during the closure period was set out. The purpose of this preparation was to maintain an existing audience relationship while continuing to develop new communities of interest, particularly among young people, through education-related projects.

Having established a dialogue with the writer John Retallack when his company performed *Hannah and Hannah* at the building in 2002, the pavilion commissioned Retallack to write a new play that reflected upon his observations of and discussions with people at the building. The result was *Ballroom* (2004), a play that tracks the lives of four elderly ballroom dancers meeting for the first time at a tea dance and reminiscing on their individual stories through the experience of dance. The production toured the United Kingdom during the summer of 2004 with great success.

The artist Bridget Smith was commissioned in 2003 to create a series of photographs that 'reflected' rather than 'documented' the process of change on which the pavilion was embarking. Over the two-year period of development, Smith captured a large number of enigmatic images that marked the transformation of a building and, in so doing, exposed its histories and its vulnerabilities as well as its magnificence.

Variety was the inaugural programme that heralded a new chapter in the De La Warr Pavilion's artistic history. While it signalled significant change for the pavilion as a new centre for contemporary art, it reflected upon a number of cultural traditions that have been associated with the building in the past and, importantly, challenged the tradition that is most often referred to as light entertainment.

It was in the year 2000, while undertaking a residency at the De La Warr Pavilion, that the artist Ian Breakwell began a discussion with Alan Haydon and Celia Davies, head of exhibitions at the pavilion, about the genre and history of non-scripted performance and its apparent influence on contemporary artists. Breakwell's lifelong interest in 'the stage' (he once had ambitions of becoming a conjuror) was harnessed by his experiences and observations of events and people at the pavilion. Over the course of several years other artists, writers and curators joined the discussion, with the result that the pavilion offered the *Variety* bill.

Variety as a programme title suggested that the pavilion was continuing the popular, even stereotyped tradition known to audiences through stage, screen and television. However, the pavilion sought to bring about a deeper understanding of a history that is not always known or appreciated and, in so doing, suggested that a significant number of contemporary artists used similar terms of reference in their work to those entertainers who once trod, or still tread, the theatrical boards. The programme provoked the thought that the brands of 'entertainment' and 'contemporary art' have a stronger bonding with popular culture than audiences are often expected or permitted to have.

After seventy years, the ambitions first set out in 1935 by the 9th Earl De La Warr can finally be delivered, albeit for the demands of a new century. The De La Warr Pavilion, putting into practice the principles established in 2000 in an ambitious artistic programme, continues as a living, breathing institution, making its mark as a significant player in the cultural life of Bexhill and also in the national and international arenas.

Whatever the outcome this period might bring in terms of celebration and success, it is clear that the pavilion's new foundations are in place and that its future, as a major independent institution, can remain focused on its new cultural purpose.

Alan Haydon is director of the De La Warr Pavilion.

LAURA FORD
The Great Indoors

Opposite, top left Bollywood Brass performs on the pavilion bandstand as part of *Jour de Fête* in 2003.

Opposite, top right The Big Spin, a skateboarding and BMX event held at the pavilion in 2005, was developed in partnership with local retailer The Source and Bexhill High School.

Opposite, centre left An exhibition of Michael Danner's photographs was staged in Gallery 2 in 2000, demonstrating the pavilion's commitment to profiling new and emerging artists.

Opposite, centre right Laura Ford's installation *The Great Indoors* (2002–2003) challenged visitors' perceptions of the familiar and unfamiliar.

Opposite, bottom The restoration now enables large-scale works to be shown. Jo Bruton's painting *Capitaine Can Can*, measuring 26 m (84 ft) wide, was featured in Gallery 1 in 2005.

Above New technologies, new facilities: the pavilion's contemporary programme attracts audiences from across the region and beyond.

Right In 2002 the pavilion participated in *The Big Draw*, a national drawing event aimed at encouraging people of all ages to discover their artistic skills.

photographic essay by bridget smith

Page 157 North staircase: The use of
cantilevers allows curved glass to extend
the full height of the north staircase,
so that it seems almost to float in the air.

Pages 158–59 South elevation:
Flat planes, steel balustrade, curved
glass: the pavilion is every inch
a Modernist ideal.

Page 160, top Foyer: New seating
hardly imposes on the entrance foyer's
expanse of terrazzo flooring, while the
pavilion's new shop is neatly installed
to blend in with its surroundings.

Page 160, bottom Restaurant: Just like the
pavilion's original PLAN furniture, tubular-
steel seating allows light to penetrate into
the heart of the new restaurant.

Page 161, top South stairs: Restoration
has meant preserving the best of the
past: nowhere is this better demonstrated
than in the sweep of Mendelsohn's south
staircase and the colours of Alvar Aalto's
original chairs.

Page 161, bottom Restaurant exterior:
Restoration has seen the original space
for the sun parlour return. Visitors are
now able to eat al fresco during the
summer months.

Pages 162–63 Roof-top foyer:
Like a look-out on the world, the top-floor
landing provides a stunning, 180-degree
vista on the way out to the reopened
roof terrace.

Page 164 North entrance: Mendelsohn's
use of lettering on buildings became one
of his trademark touches. The restoration
recognizes this, picking out the pavilion's
name in neon.

author's acknowledgements

I would like to express my grateful thanks to the many colleagues, experts, friends of the De La Warr Pavilion and kindred spirits without whom the research and writing of this book would have been impossible.

To Alan Haydon for his confidence and belief that I was the right man for the job. To Jill Theis for her incredible mind and unwavering support. To the many people who pointed me in the right directions with their personal memories: Jack Seabrook, John Dowling, Richard Rogers, Peter Palumbo, Kitty Giles – thank you all. To the dear, departed Esther Mendelsohn Joseph and her daughter Daria, who brought so many memories of their father and grandfather to life in San Francisco. To Alan Powers for his expert eye; Itta Greenberg for her fountain of knowledge; and John McAslan and Adam Brown for their architectural guidance. To John Bratby for his Californian hospitality; Leslie Brissett and Fran McKeown, who held the fort while I wrote; Genevieve Hilton-Harwood, who managed my mountain of files; and Laurence Malice, who gave me the break that I needed. To Celia Davies at the pavilion and Julian Honer and Claire Chandler at Merrell for their wonderful professionalism. To my two children, Paris and Carson, for their patience with Dad. And last but by no means least, to my sister, Josephine Sams, for being there just when I needed her.

Alastair Fairley

chronology of the de la warr pavilion

1930 A report by Adams, Thomson & Fry proposes the construction of a 'Music Pavilion and Enlarged Band Enclosure' as part of a larger development plan for Bexhill. Bexhill Corporation commissions Tubbs & Messer, a local firm of architects, to develop the proposals.

1932 The 9th Earl De La Warr is elected the first socialist mayor of Bexhill.

1933 A competition is launched for the design and construction of the pavilion.

February 1934 The design by Erich Mendelsohn and Serge Chermayeff wins the competition, announced in *The Architects' Journal*.

April 1934 The Ministry of Health launches an inquiry to approve a loan for construction.

Mendelsohn and Chermayeff produce a model of the pavilion project, including the proposed amendments of the pergola, swimming pool and pier.

September 1934 The Ministry of Health approves a £78,412 loan for construction.

January 1935 Construction starts on the new pavilion.

March 1935 George V and Queen Mary visit the pavilion building site.

May 1935 Earl De La Warr lays the pavilion foundation plaque.

July 1935 The Lord Mayor of London visits the construction site as part of an official visit to launch the electrification of the railway line from London Victoria to Hastings.

October 1935 The council abandons the pavilion swimming pool project, and defers the decisions on the statue and the pergola.

The council agrees to name the pavilion after Earl De La Warr.

12 December 1935 The De La Warr Pavilion is opened by the Duke and Duchess of York.

March 1936 The council criticizes the pavilion's music policy and abandons the symphony concerts. Matthew Forsyth, the entertainments director, resigns to concentrate on the repertory company, the Forsyth Players.

The pavilion appears in a Southern Railway promotional poster.

April 1936 The council announces rate rises and is accused of "squandermania" by residents. Expenditure on the pavilion takes the blame. A committee of inquiry is launched to investigate accounts.

July 1936 Mendelsohn and Chermayeff publish new plans for further work on the pavilion scheme, to include a cinema and a hotel.

October 1936 An investigation into the pavilion accounts is commissioned from the district auditor. The council is found to have managed the pavilion's finances satisfactorily.

The Concours d'élégance car rally is held on the pavilion's terrace.

November 1936 The pavilion repertory company premieres *The Millionairess*, a new play by George Bernard Shaw. Shaw visits the pavilion for the premiere.

1937 The pavilion model is displayed at the Royal Academy's Exhibition of British Architecture.

The prime minister, Neville Chamberlain, visits the pavilion.

The first Design and Industries Association conference is held at the pavilion.

1938 The council appoints the Forsyth Players to undertake forty-three weeks of repertory theatre during the year.

The council proposes the removal of the library and its replacement with an extended dance hall area.

September 1939 War is declared. The pavilion closes for two weeks under government restrictions.

October 1939 The Ministry of Defence requisitions the first floor of the pavilion for its southern command operations centre.

November 1939–August 1940 The pavilion remains open for plays and concerts but to an increasingly limited degree, due to dwindling audiences.

May 1940 Fire guts the Metropole Hotel.

July 1940 The government bans recreational visits to the coast. The pavilion closes its repertory theatre programme.

A major evacuation of schoolchildren from Bexhill takes place.

August 1940 The pavilion closes its restaurant and ends the musical trio performances.

September 1940 A bomb damages the pavilion's west wall and auditorium and severely damages the Metropole Hotel.

The Rotary Club persuades the council to reopen the damaged pavilion, and agrees to promote events for armed forces and prisoner of war welfare funds.

December 1940 The Rotary Club hosts the first of many wartime dances at the pavilion, with a military jazz band.

March 1941 The Rotary Club launches a programme of boxing tournaments at the pavilion.

August 1941 The people of Bexhill donate almost 60 tonnes of scrap metal during the National Salvage Programme, possibly including the pavilion's roundel nameplates.

The Women's Voluntary Service opens the British Restaurant at the pavilion.

1942 Bexhill is subjected to regular 'tip-and-run' bombing raids.

1944 In a single day, 480 flying bombs are tracked passing over Bexhill. Several land, causing damage to the town.

The council commissions a report on war damage and dilapidations from Mendelsohn's assistant, Hannes Schreiner. The report includes a proposal for the development of a new dance hall, two new bars and a soda fountain.

May 1945 Peace in Europe is declared. The council reinstates the repertory theatre and a musical programme. Twenty-eight thousand people visit repertory performances in a ten-week period.

1946 The pavilion's west wall is torn down and rebuilt, and repairs to the auditorium are carried out.

1947 The pavilion launches an annual summer show, with a repertory theatre programme the rest of the year.

January 1949 The Royal Philharmonic Orchestra, conducted by Sir Thomas Beecham, plays at the pavilion.

1951 The pavilion hosts its first *Starlight Rendezvous* summer show, which runs for ten years. The comedian Freddie Frinton plays to audiences of almost 62,000 over the season.

1954 The first British package holidays to Spain's Costa del Sol are launched.

The Marine Mansions hotel is demolished, the first of many to disappear over the next ten years.

1955 The council undertakes renovations to the pavilion's interior. The sun parlour is enclosed, the reading room is extended to form a small function room and dance hall, and the lounge bar is relocated.

1960 The pavilion launches a programme of summer music festivals. The Hallé Orchestra, conducted by Sir John Barbirolli, headlines.

1962 The council commissions Henry Ward & Partners to prepare a report on proposed alterations to the building. It accepts the findings. Work starts immediately.

1963 A new lounge bar is constructed on the first floor. Goods access requirements lead to the renovation of the lecture hall, including the construction of a false ceiling. Screens are constructed between the lounge bar and the function room. New toilets are installed and the manager's office relocated. The dance floor in the restaurant is removed, and a self-service cafeteria is created. The new kitchens reduce the restaurant size. Potted plants are introduced to the pavilion's rooms and staircase.

1964 The pavilion posts record financial losses.

1966 The Queen and the Duke of Edinburgh visit the pavilion.

1967 The interior is redecorated in a more intimate and domestic style. The first-floor function room is redecorated with wood and carpeted, and renamed the Elizabeth room. The lecture room is reduced in size and renamed the Edinburgh room. The bar is wallpapered and carpeted.

1969 The pavilion's repertory company posts a record £29,716 loss for the year.

1971 The council proposes the siting of a new lift in the centre of the staircase. It writes to Chermayeff, asking for the original plans. He objects strongly to the proposal.

A restoration programme starts to replace the steel window frames with timber ones.

1972 A lift is installed in the auditorium foyer. The foyer and entrance hall are redecorated with flock wallpaper.

The east-wing roof is replaced.

1973 New government fire-escape regulations force the closure of the roof terrace to the public. New fire screens are erected at the main entrance and on the first and second floors. A ramp for disabled visitors is added to the entrance. A new goods yard is created on the north wall to house beer barrels and provide a staff entrance. The second floor is closed to the public, and the manager's offices are relocated there.

1974 Bexhill Council ceases operation under a new local government act. The new Rother District Council assumes ownership of the pavilion.

1975 The cafeteria is renovated to provide self-service catering with fixed plastic seating. A screen is constructed to separate it from the waiter-service restaurant.

The pavilion ceases its repertory theatre, replacing it with an entertainments programme of 'one-off' shows.

New boilers are installed.

1977 A stone sculpture is added to the entrance lobby to commemorate the Queen's silver jubilee.

1978 The west-wing auditorium roof is replaced. A new bandstand is constructed on the south terrace.

1982 A new catwalk system is constructed for the auditorium flies.

1984 The rusting south staircase steelwork is repaired.

1985 The pavilion celebrates its golden anniversary.

The proposal to replace the entrance doors is dropped on grounds of cost. A lobby group at the council is formed to promote the conservation of the building.

An article appears in the *RIBA Journal* bemoaning the poor state of the pavilion.

The British Steel Industry hails the pavilion as a "structural steel classic".

1986 The council secures Grade I listing for the pavilion.

1987 A new toilet and cloakroom are constructed on the ground floor of the auditorium foyer.

A major Mendelsohn retrospective exhibition is held at the pavilion.

The October hurricane causes major damage to the auditorium roof.

1988 The ground-floor cafeteria and restaurant are redecorated, and vertical blinds are installed.

1989 The Edinburgh room is redecorated in a 1930s style.

The Pavilion Trust is launched to restore the building, promote its significance and undertake an educational programme.

Cracks emerge on the south elevation. The council commissions a structural survey and rejects the Pavilion Trust's recommendation for a full strategy report.

1990 The council commissions repair work to the south elevation by its own architects.

The Pavilion Trust commissions its own restoration strategy report from architect John McAslan of Troughton McAslan.

Peter Palumbo, chairman of the Arts Council, visits the pavilion and supports the trust's work.

1991 Initial repair work exposes major structural damage to the south elevation.

1992 The Pavilion Trust publishes a Stage I restoration strategy report from John McAslan, which is adopted by Rother Council. The council then appoints Troughton McAslan to undertake works, part-funded by English Heritage.

The trust launches an artist- and architect-in-residence programme.

The trust launches an appeal to restore the roundel signs, the flagpole and the south staircase light fitting.

A cache of original Alvar Aalto furniture is discovered in an attic room.

1993 Restoration work to the south elevation is completed, at a cost of £420,000.

Restoration of the south staircase light fitting, funded by the Pavilion Trust, begins.

The trust commissions a Stage II restoration strategy report from Troughton McAslan to determine the future restoration strategy, fundraising and management of the pavilion. The council adopts the report's proposals.

The council commissions a report from consultants; it recommends that the pavilion should be used as a "living art gallery".

The trust develops a pavilion education resource pack for schools in conjunction with the Construction Industry Training Board.

1994 The fully repaired flagpole and staircase light fitting are restored to the building.

The trust launches a restoration programme for the Alvar Aalto furniture.

An education room is created on the first floor for school visits to the pavilion.

1995 The first-floor interior restoration is completed. The Edinburgh room is removed and the lecture theatre restored to create a new gallery space. The Elizabeth room decoration is stripped away. A new lounge bar area is created. The costs of £249,000 are met by the district and county councils, the Foundation for Sport and the Arts, and other organizations.

The council completes a new arts strategy that highlights opportunities for the visual arts at the pavilion.

The council makes an £8,900,000 bid to the Arts Council Lottery for redevelopment works.

The pavilion's sixtieth-birthday celebrations include exhibitions, talks, concerts and a visit by Esther Mendelsohn Joseph, the architect's daughter.

1996 The Pavilion Trust launches a programme of guided tours around the building, as well as design workshops for schools in conjunction with RIBA South East, and talks and lectures for groups.

Arts Council England turns down the Lottery bid, but provides £500,000 to develop the plan further.

Caroline Collier is appointed general manager of the pavilion.

1997 A new scheme for redevelopment is proposed by John McAslan + Partners.

The roundels are restored to the building's south and east walls.

1998 The council makes a further Lottery bid to Arts Council England for £16,500,000 to establish the pavilion as a centre for the arts.

The Pavilion Trust purchases the original Edward Wadsworth sketch for the pavilion's mural for £12,000. It raises £75,000 from sponsors to construct the new pavilion bandstand. The architect Niall McLaughlin wins the competition to create the design.

1999 Arts Council England rejects the council's Lottery funding bid but offers a further £120,000 to 're-scope' the application.

The new council invites expressions of interest from private operators to take over the running of the building.

The auditorium is refurbished by John McAslan + Partners to provide new seating and lighting.

Alan Haydon is appointed director of the pavilion.

October 2000 The council drops its plans for the private operation of the pavilion.

New bids are submitted to Arts Council England and the Heritage Lottery Fund.

2001 A new bandstand is erected on the pavilion terrace.

April 2002 Arts Council England awards a £4,100,000 Lottery grant towards the pavilion's new proposals. The Heritage Lottery Fund awards £1,900,000 towards restoration and repair.

The Pavilion Trust winds up its affairs in preparation for the new charitable trust.

The bandstand design receives a special award from the RIBA for design excellence.

The bandstand education project is accepted as a module for teaching design and technology as part of the National Curriculum.

2003 The De La Warr Pavilion Charitable Trust formally takes over the ownership and management of the pavilion.

2004 The building closes. Comprehensive restoration work starts under the leadership of John McAslan + Partners.

A further £2,000,000 is raised towards the redevelopment from a number of public and private sources.

15 October 2005 The De La Warr Pavilion reopens to the public as a new centre for the contemporary arts in south-east England. Some 10,000 people visit the pavilion over the first weekend.

12 December 2005 On the seventieth anniversary of the building's opening, the 11th Earl De La Warr officially reopens the pavilion.

further reading

Published Writings by Mendelsohn

Amerika: Bilderbuch eines Architekten [America: Picturebook of an Architect], Berlin (Rudolf Mosse) 1926

Russland, Europa, Amerika: Ein architektonischer Querschnitt [Russia, Europe, America: An Architectural Cross-section], Berlin (Rudolf Mosse) 1929

Erich Mendelsohn: Das Gesamtschaffen des Architekten – Skizzen, Entwürfe, Bauten [Erich Mendelsohn: Complete Works of the Architect – Sketches, Designs, Buildings], Berlin (Rudolf Mosse) 1930

Neues Haus, neue Welt [New House, New World], Berlin (Rudolf Mosse) 1932

Der schöpferische Sinn der Krise [The Creative Sense of Crisis], Berlin (Bruno Cassirer) 1932

'Visions of an Architect', *Magazine of Art*, vol. 38, no. 8, December 1945, pp. 307–310

'Background to Design', *Architectural Forum*, vol. 98, no. 4, April 1953, pp. 106–107

Unpublished Lectures by Mendelsohn

Original texts of lectures cited are all in the Erich and Louise Mendelsohn Papers, 1887–1992, Getty Research Institute, Los Angeles, California.

'The Laws of Modern Architecture', New York 1924

'The Fate of This Hour', Brussels, 6 April 1933

'Rebuilding the World', London 1937, Edinburgh 1938

'What is and What Ought to Be', London, April 1937

'Palestine and the Mediterranean: The Cultural Impact of 2000 B.C. and 2000 A.D.', New York 1943

Writings about Mendelsohn

Mario Federico Roggero, *Il contributo di Mendelsohn alla evoluzione dell'architettura moderna* [Mendelsohn's Contribution to the Evolution of Modern Architecture], Milan (Libreria editrice politecnica Tamburini) 1952

Arnold Whittick, *Eric Mendelsohn*, 2nd edn, London (Leonard Hill) and New York (F.W. Dodge) 1956

Wolf von Eckardt, *Eric Mendelsohn*, New York (George Braziller) 1960

Erich Mendelsohn: Letters of an Architect, ed. Oskar Beyer, trans. Geoffrey Strachan, London and New York (Abelard-Schuman) 1967

Erich Mendelsohn, exhib. cat. by Julius Posener and Peter Pfankuch, Berlin, Akademie der Künste, 1968

The Drawings of Eric Mendelsohn, exhib. cat. by Susan King, Berkeley, University of California Art Museum, 1969

Ita Heinze-Mühleib, *Erich Mendelsohn, Bauten und Projekte in Palästina (1934–1941)* [Erich Mendelsohn, Buildings and Projects in Palestine (1934–1941)], Munich (Scaneg) 1986

Erich Mendelsohn 1887–1953, exhib. cat., ed. Jeremy Brook and Nasser Golzari, Bexhill on Sea and London, 1987

Erich Mendelsohn, 1887–1953: Ideen, Bauten, Projekte [Erich Mendelsohn, 1887–1953: Ideas, Buildings, Projects], exhib. cat., ed. Sigrid Achenbach, Berlin, Staatliche Museen Preußischer Kulturbesitz, 1987

Erich Mendelsohn, 1887–1953, exhib. cat. by Peter Blundell-Jones *et al.*, Bexhill on Sea and London, 1987–88

Birkin Haward, 'Recollections of the Mendelsohn & Chermayeff Practice, London and Jerusalem 1934–1938', unpublished work, recorded in 1988, in De La Warr Pavilion Archive

Hans Rudolf Morgenthaler, *The Early Sketches of German Architect Erich Mendelsohn (1887–1953): No Compromise with Reality*, Lewiston NY and Lampeter (Edwin Mellen Press) 1992

Kathleen James, *Erich Mendelsohn and the Architecture of German Modernism*, Cambridge and New York (Cambridge University Press) 1997

Regina Stephan (ed.), *Eric Mendelsohn: Architect, 1887–1953*, New York (Monacelli Press) 1999

Bruno Zevi, *Erich Mendelsohn: The Complete Works*, trans. by Lucinda Byatt, Basel (Birkhäuser) 1999

Published Writings by Chermayeff

Colour and its Application to Modern Building, London (Nobel Chemical Finishes) 1936

Shape of Privacy, Cambridge MA (Harvard University Graduate School of Design) 1961

(With Christopher Alexander) *Community and Privacy: Toward a New Architecture of Humanism*, Garden City NY (Doubleday) 1963

(With Alexander Tzonis) *Advanced Studies in Urban Environments*, New Haven CT (Yale University Press) 1966

(With Alexander Tzonis) *Shape of Community: Realization of Human Potential*, Harmondsworth (Penguin) 1971

Published Articles by Chermayeff

Chermayeff spent much of his life contributing articles to various publications worldwide. This is a selection of some of his more relevant works.

'The Modern Approach to Architecture and its Equipment', *The Architects' Journal*, vol. 77, 8 March 1933, pp. 337–80

'Thoughts on Modern Architecture', *RIBA Journal*, vol. 40, 8 July 1933, p. 689

(With J.M. Richards) 'A Hundred Years Ahead: Forecasting the Coming Century', *The Architects' Journal*, vol. 81, 10 January 1935, pp. 79–86

'The Architect's Duty to the Modern World', *The Builder*, vol. 150, 24 January 1936, p. 205

'Modern Art and Architecture', *RIBA Journal*, vol. 44, 9 January 1937, p. 209

'Architecture at the Chicago Institute of Design', *L'Architecture d'aujourd'hui*, vol. 10, February 1950, pp. 50–56

'The Architectural Condition', *The Architectural Association Journal*, vol. 80, July 1964, pp. 45–50

'The Shape of Humanism', *Arts and Society* [Pennsylvania State University], vol. 7, 1971, pp. 517–31

'An Explosive Revolution', *Architectural Review*, vol. 166, November 1979, p. 309

Writings about Chermayeff

'The Makers of Broadcasting House', *Country Life*, 28 May 1932, p. 603

Richard Plunz (ed.), *Design and the Public Good: Selected Writings 1930–1980 by Serge Chermayeff*, Cambridge MA and London (MIT Press) 1982

Barbara Tilson, 'The Modern Art Department, Waring & Gillow, 1928–1931', *Journal of the Decorative Arts Society*, no. 8, 1984, pp. 40–49

Peter Blake, *No Place Like Utopia: Modern Architecture and the Company We Kept*, New York (Knopf) 1993

Alan Powers, 'Spirit of Modernism', *The Architects' Journal*, vol. 202, no. 15, 19 October 1995, pp. 24–26

Alan Powers, *Serge Chermayeff: Designer, Architect, Teacher*, London (RIBA Publications) 2001

Serge Chermayeff, 1900–1996: The Shape of Modern Living, exhib. cat. by Alan Powers, Cambridge, Kettle's Yard, 2001

Writings about the 9th Earl De La Warr

A.J.P. Taylor, *English History, 1914–1945* (The Oxford History of England, vol. 15), Oxford (Clarendon Press) 1965, p. 452

Belinda Kidd and Jenna Kumiega, *Arts Festivals in the South East* (South East Arts Board) 1997

Alastair Fairley, *Bucking the Trend: The Life and Times of the Ninth Earl De La Warr*, Bexhill on Sea (Pavilion Trust) 2001

Writings about the De La Warr Pavilion and Related Subjects

The following sources are listed in chronological order and are not exhaustive. Bexhill Library holds a microfiche archive of the local newspaper, the *Bexhill Observer* (formerly the *Bexhill-on-Sea Observer*), which has carried reports on the pavilion from 1934 to the present day; only principal articles are highlighted here. A large body of archive material is held by the De La Warr Pavilion itself and can be inspected on request.

Architect and Building News: a number of short articles on the 'Competition for a New Entertainments Pavilion, Bexhill on Sea', September–October 1933

'Notice for the Competition for a New Entertainments Pavilion, Bexhill-on-Sea', *The Architects' Journal*, vol. 78, 7 September 1933, p. 290

Thomas Tait, 'The Winner's Report: Design Placed First', *The Architects' Journal*, vol. 79, 8 February 1934, pp. 214–18

'Progress with Construction of the New Entertainments Pavilion, Bexhill-on-Sea', *Building*, July 1935, pp. 276–83

Review: 'The De La Warr Pavilion, Bexhill', *The Architects' Journal*, vol. 82, 12 December 1935, pp. 872–84

'Enchanting Smiles of Popular Duchess', *Bexhill-on-Sea Observer*, 14 December 1935, p.1

Review: *Architect and Building News*, vol. 144, 20 and 27 December 1935, pp. 343–47, 372–75

'The De La Warr Pavilion, Bexhill-on-Sea' [including a long note provided by the structural engineers], *The Builder*, vol. 149, 20 December 1935, pp.1104–109, 1111

Working Details: 'The De La Warr Pavilion, Bexhill', *The Architects' Journal*, vol. 82, 26 December 1935, pp. 957–60

Arnold Whittick, 'The De La Warr Pavilion, Bexhill-on-Sea', *Building*, January 1936

'De La Warr Pavilion, Bexhill-on-Sea', *Country Life*, vol. 79, no. 2039, 15 February 1936, p. xxvii

'How the Pavilion Should Be Run', *Bexhill-on-Sea Observer*, 28 March 1936, p.10

Serge Chermayeff (as Peter Maitland), 'Leisure at the Seaside: IV. The Architect' [with illustrations by László Moholy-Nagy], *Architectural Review*, vol. 80, July 1936, pp.18–28

'Music for All', *Bexhill-on-Sea Observer*, 16 November 1936, p. 8

Modern Architecture in England, exhib. cat. by Henry-Russell Hitchcock, New York, Museum of Modern Art, 1937

J.M. Richards, *An Introduction to Modern Architecture*, Harmondsworth (Penguin) 1940

Hannes Schreiner, *Report on War Damage and Dilapidations and Suggestions for Improvements and Additions for the Entertainments Committee of the Borough of Bexhill*, Borough of Bexhill, September 1944

The War in East Sussex, Hastings (F.J. Parsons) 1945. First published in *Sussex Express & County Herald*, August 1945

'Major Extension Plans', *Bexhill-on-Sea Observer*, 15 January 1955, p.13

Malcolm Higgs, 'Felix James Samuely, 1902–1959', *Journal of the Architectural Association*, vol. 76, June 1960, pp. 2–31

Ralph Barton White, *Qualitative Studies of Buildings: The De La Warr Pavilion, Bexhill-on-Sea and the Gilbey Building, Oval Road, London, N.W.1* (National Building Studies Special Report no. 39), London (HMSO) 1966

'Wartime Gave De La Warr Pavilion its Finest Hour', *Bexhill-on-Sea Observer*, 7 October 1967, p. 21

L.J. Bartley, *The Story of Bexhill*, Bexhill on Sea (F.J. Parsons) 1971

Spike Milligan, *Adolf Hitler: My Part in his Downfall*, London (Joseph) 1971

Tim Benton, *The De La Warr Pavilion: A Type for the 1930s* (from fourteen papers given at the second conference on Twentieth-Century Design History), London (Design Council Publications) 1977

Buildings for Further Study, Open University Summer School Booklet, 1979, in De La Warr Pavilion Archive

Jonathan Glancey and David Hamilton Eddy, 'Mendelsohn Chermayeff All at Sea', *RIBA Journal*, vol. 92, September 1985, pp. 30–36

Barbara Tilson, 'Form and Function', *Building Design*, no. 864, 4 December 1987, pp.15–17

Russell Stevens and Peter Willis, 'Earl De La Warr and the Competition for the Bexhill Pavilion', *Architectural History*, vol. 33, 1990, pp.134–65

Kenneth Powell, 'Shame and Scandal in Bexhill-on-Sea', *Daily Telegraph*, 12 July 1990, p.14

Rory Coonan, 'Will the Barbarians Triumph at Bexhill?', *The Observer* (arts supplement), 26 August 1990

David Radtke, 'A Princess in Rags: A History of the Bexhill Pavilion 1935–1990', unpublished diss., Brighton Polytechnic 1991, in De La Warr Pavilion Archive

'Bexhill's Bauhaus-on-Sea', *The Independent*, 11 December 1991, p.14

John McAslan, *Restoration Strategy for the De La Warr Pavilion*, Bexhill on Sea (Pavilion Trust) 1993

Fred Gray (ed.), *Bexhill Voices*, Falmer (Centre for Continuing Education, University of Sussex) 1994

Kenneth Powell, 'Restoring a Milestone of Modernism', *The Architects' Journal*, vol. 199, 16 February 1994, pp. 35–44

John Dowling, 'The Gamble: Changes at the De La Warr Pavilion', *Bexhill Observer*, 15 September 1995, p.11

John McAslan, 'Restoring a Modernist Masterpiece', *Conservation Bulletin*, issue 27, November 1995, pp. 5–7

S.L. Benson, 'The De La Warr Pavilion: Meeting the Needs of Social Change (1933–1996)', *Interior Architecture & Design*, 26 February 1996

Kenneth Powell, *John McAslan*, London (Thames & Hudson) 1999

'The Story of Bexhill and the De La Warr Pavilion', recorded interview with Peter Evenden (1920–1998), Bexhill on Sea (Pavilion Trust) 1999

Jonathan Glancey, 'And They Want to Turn This into a Pub?', *The Guardian*, 27 March 2000, p.10

Alastair Fairley, *Turning the Tide: A Short History of the Pavilion Trust, 1989–2002*, Bexhill on Sea (Pavilion Trust) 2002

Alastair Fairley, 'Band Aid: The De La Warr Pavilion Bandstand', *Times Educational Supplement*, 28 June 2002, pp. 24–25

Alastair Fairley, 'Let There Be Light', *Independent Magazine*, 13 July 2002, pp. 52–53

Jonathan Glancey, 'On the Waterfront', *The Guardian*, 13 January 2003, pp.12–13

Kenneth Powell, *Culture of Building: The Architecture of John McAslan + Partners*, London and New York (Merrell) 2004

Fiona McCarthy, 'Pleasure Palaces', *The Guardian*, 6 August 2005, p.16

Tom Dyckhoff, 'Oh, We Do Like to Be Beside the (Modernist) Seaside', *The Times*, 23 August 2005, section 2, pp.14–15

'De La Warr: The Fall and Rise', *Building Design*, 14 October 2005, pp.14–17

index

Page numbers in *italic* refer to illustrations

picture credits